BEING
PERFECTLY
IMPERFECT

Discover the Brilliance of
YOU

By

Tracey Ward
BEng(Civil), GDip.Psych

For my beautiful mother, Peggy.

Tracey Ward

The woman you were always meant to be…

…who somehow got lost along the way by dedication to work, family, a partner, cooking, washing, taking pets to the vet, baking cakes, and fundraisers.

Introduction

One of my earliest memories is being carried into my home from the car by a man. I remember holding a small plastic horse and being very pleased with my new toy. This would be the only time I recall being held by my father. In fact, it's possibly the only time a man held me until I started dating. Now, don't get me wrong; this isn't a sob story or a "woe is me" tale—far from it. But the absence of a father or any influential male figure in my life shaped my world very differently from many other women, and I feel it's key to understanding this book.

I was brought up by my beautiful mother, who was a forty-year-old single parent in the 1960s. "Oh, do you have to put that in, dear?" I can hear my grandmother say. "The shame of it." My mum was a trailblazer, ahead of her time. She got her pilot's license in the forties and did crazy aerobatics. War was a time of freedom for her; life was full of adventure. But when I came along, that freedom disappeared, and the constraints of societal norms and the pressures of being a single working mother hemmed her in.

For most of my childhood, I lived with my mum, grandmother, and grandfather. This enabled my mum to go to work to support the lot of us and for my grandparents, when they were able, to pick me up from school. Mum was a part of the "sandwich generation" for nearly two decades, way before the term was coined (I told you she was a trailblazer), feeling the pressures of providing and caring for both her parents and child simultaneously. Was she a special case, or was that just what women did? In my home, my mum did everything. She worked, shopped, cooked, cleaned, painted, decorated, and fixed the car. She took us on outings to the doctor and dentist, tended to our wounds, and tidied up our messes. During my childhood, as my mum did everything, my grandfather, who was in his eighties, watched cricket and tended his roses; he was too tired to deal with a lively child. My grandmother, for the most part, incessantly cut up or set household objects aflame. My grandmother had dementia and felt like another child in the house—but the "naughty one"—and kept us all on constant high alert.

What I saw in my mum was a woman who cared, had endless compassion for others, and who was always giving and never complaining. "Lucky you," you might say, and yes, we were very lucky to have her. But what I also saw from an extremely early age was she had no life, she was constantly tired, and always stressed about money while trying to hold everything and everyone together, and ultimately, paid too high a price and died before meeting her beautiful grandchildren.

So, what did I learn?

I learnt two things. First, women can do anything: fly planes, change the oil in a car, hang wallpaper, bake cakes, put out fires, and still follow the plot in a TV show.

The second thing I learnt is when women don't look after themselves, it's not only unhealthy for them but their loved ones as well. In my childhood, Mum worried about where the money was coming from, and I worried about her.

This book is for all the beautiful women out there who look after and care for people both at work and at home. It's to help gain your life back and find moments of respite, time to recharge your batteries, find joy in life again, and still maintain the fulfilling role of caregiver. This book will take you through a step-by-step process to help you reconnect with the perfectly imperfect you and start looking after yourself. After all, if *you* don't look after you, who will?

The good news is, researchers have found if you start looking after yourself better, it increases, not decreases, your compassion and energy levels (Neff et al. 2007, 139-54). Plus, for lovely, mature women who have reached menopause, it helps relieve symptoms (Brown et al. 2015, 293–99). So, self-compassion is a win for you *and* those around you.

In terms of how you can get the most out of this book, each chapter deals with a different topic, such as making time for yourself, setting boundaries, and bringing fun back. Each chapter has activities designed to enhance your life and help you reconnect with the woman you were always meant to be. Believe me, these activities work. I use them personally and give them to my clients, and I've been coaching women for over twenty years.

This is where you make a choice. You can whizz through all of the chapters in this book then search for your next panacea on Amazon, or you can take your time, do the activities, re-read the chapters, and surprise yourself with the wonderful changes occurring in your life. Whichever you choose, it's lovely to have you on the journey with me.

Live, love, sparkle.

Tracey

P.S. All stories in this book are true. Names and places have been changed to respect the privacy of others.

Chapter 1: Save Time to Make Time for You

This chapter and the one that follows are both designed to help find more time for yourself. If you already have lots of free time, don't worry too much about the activities; just reading the concepts will be a timely refresher and perhaps provide you with a technique to share with someone you feel would benefit from having more time for themselves.

We'll discuss saving yourself time both at home and work, which is a powerful self-compassion technique. Don't worry if you live on your own. At first, you might think, *How can I save time at home? I have to do everything myself.* Trust me; there are cunning ways to help you save oodles of time. It's exciting! The same is true if you work on your own. We just have to think laterally. I'm here to guide you.

Let's start by delving into the world of self-compassion.

Think of the most recent time you helped someone in a tight spot who just needed support. How would you describe your style of care? After reading through these descriptions over the next few sections, you'll be able to see how you categorise yourself as a helper, giver, etc. Now, take a moment to think of all the people you have helped recently. How did you do it?

- Did you help out with tasks?
- Were you a great listener and counsellor?

- Were you a compassionate hugger, hand-holder, or maybe there just because they needed someone to be with

You can apply all of these compassion techniques to your family and friends. How you help others is how you will start helping yourself. You'll love your life when you master all of these techniques and practise them on your beautiful self. Let's look at how your compassion style translates into self-compassion.

1. The Helper

The helper is a lovely person who supports others by "doing stuff." They will drop in on you with a homemade meal, take your kids swimming, or do a shop for you. These helpers understand the importance of easing up your workload pressure when you're stressed or ill. Easing this excess pressure is paramount in giving the other party time to heal. It's no different than when you tear a muscle at the gym—allowing yourself to mend is a must. In fact, you don't have to be injured or sick to benefit from a break. Elite athletes have recovery time. They don't train every day, and research shows rest provides great physical and psychological benefits to their performance (Quinn 2020). If it's beneficial for elite athletes, it has to be beneficial for us. We might not run as fast or lift as heavy of weights, but if these elite athletes saw what we juggled every day, they would be exhausted. We need time to recuperate.

If you can accept that lightening a friend's workload will help her recuperate and bounce back, the same logic must apply to ourselves. The question is: how can you reduce the pressure on yourself in your everyday life?

The reality is, not every task has to be done today, and often it doesn't have to be done by you. Similarly, not every task necessarily needs perfection. "Good enough is good enough," and sometimes the task doesn't need to be done at all! As women, we're very good at taking on tasks we shouldn't. If you've ever used the phrase, "Oh, *I'll* just do it then!" you know what I mean. It's time to ease up on your workload.

You're going to take a look at *all* your tasks and see which you can **d**elegate, **s**implify, or **d**ump (DSD). Before you start (and I can already hear you saying, "But, but, but you don't understand; it's just not possible! I'm busy for a reason! I have a bucket load to do!"), let me expand on this concept, as it is a *very* important foundation of self-compassion.

Every woman can delegate, simplify, or dump some of her tasks. The only person standing in the way of this happening is you. Just as an example, let's look at cooking, something most of us do daily.

Delegate: Give yourself permission not to cook all the time.

Delegate cooking to someone else one or two evenings a week. This will empower them and help them build a whole new skillset.

Simplify: No need for Le Cordon Bleu meals every night.

If I'm cooking for myself at night, my favourite meal is a sweet potato cooked in the microwave; green salad consisting of a bit of lettuce, tomato, cucumber, some feta cheese, and olives; and a tin of tuna. No pots and pans to wash up, and it all fits on one plate, to boot. If you replace the tuna with a ready roasted chicken from the store, you have a simple family meal in minutes with barely any washing up.

Dump: Order in (you've got to love Uber Eats), or go out for dinner.

There are lots of tasks around the home that can be simplified or not done at all. I, for example, don't fold or iron clothes, nor do I pair socks (I buy a load of the same socks in one go, which helps). I don't make beds or insist my teenagers do so, as it just seems like a waste of time.

Now, you may have read this and been horrified, and that's okay. No matter your reaction, step back for a moment and think. Whether you iron, fold, pair your socks, or make your bed, do these tasks make you happy? My mum loved ironing; she found it therapeutic. Weird, as far as I was concerned, but hey, isn't it great we're all different? If the tasks you do day in and day out genuinely make you happy, keep doing them. If they don't, create free time for yourself by delegating, simplifying, or dumping the task. Get the idea?

Exercise 1:

Now, make a list of *all* the tasks you do, large or small, from feeding the cat to washing and shopping. Build this list step by step over the week; it's important. When you have compiled your full list and written it down on paper, reflect. It probably explains why you feel tired all the time and never get to the gym. As much as we would each like to think we are Superwoman, we aren't. Instead, we are *super women* who are about to be very kind and compassionate to ourselves!

If you work outside the home, have a separate list of *all* of your work tasks. Refer back to your job description and what you are actually paid to do to help keep perspective on what you realistically should and shouldn't be doing. Again, invest time in doing this task. It may take some contemplation and conversation with others.

Complete one list before the other. Start with the most draining, be it work or home life. It's best not to do them at the same time, as it might be too overwhelming. One step at a time.

Looking at your work tasks, I'm here to tell you, just working hard doesn't get you promoted. Let me say that again: just working hard doesn't get you promoted. Instead, you need to work smart and be seen doing a great job. Being seen doing a great job is different than doing a great job, and in my twenty-five years of coaching women, I've seen way too many of them unintentionally hiding their brilliance at work. Then they wonder why the person next to them got promoted. For more information on this, have a look at my "Two Roles" vlog, as mentioned in the index (page 98).

Now, with your list of tasks in front of you, see which tasks you can delegate, simplify, or dump. For any task you identify to DSD, write down a correlated action in your diary to make sure it happens this week. Next, calculate the time you have saved; this is precious time you are going to use wisely for yourself. (See the DSD chart at the end of this chapter.)

2. The Listener and Good Counsellor

These people utilise another gorgeous compassion technique. You may be someone who patiently sits and listens to a friend or family member share their problems, suffering, or pain. You validate their feelings by helping them understand their issue is valid. You put their situation into perspective and kindly guide them along the way, helping them find solutions to their challenges. Listening to someone else without judgement is one of the most beautiful gifts you can give. In this busy world, we are rarely heard and too often judged, so to have someone take time out of their day to sit and listen without scrutiny is pure gold.

Connecting with ourselves is just as valuable. It's all about checking in, understanding, and accepting how we feel and where we are at. It took me until age fifty to realise the importance of this. I think I learnt resilience and how to cope on my own from my mother. She was very resilient. She helped others, and I don't recollect her ever asking for help; it's just what she did.

This is such a skewed view of life, thinking you have to do everything on your own and that it's a sign of weakness to ask for help. No, let me tell you, dear reader, this is not a great approach. It's exhausting. But being a slow learner myself, I had to learn the hard way.

What I've realised is many women are *too* resilient. Our tolerance levels are enormous. Any sane person would go, "Are you kidding?" But instead, we say, "That's okay. I've got this. Bring it on."

A friend of mine, Debbie, was an IT consultant. She went into companies and did all sorts of IT magic I don't pretend to understand. She was a strong, capable woman in a very male-dominated workplace. Her job was to find problems and correct them. Companies loved her, but IT departments often didn't because she exposed their failings for all to see. She was often treated badly. The corporate game-playing was awful, and I wondered how sustainable that was for her mental health in the long run. "I'm fine," she would always say when we caught up on Skype.

Years went by, and the strain was noticeably wearing on her. I challenged her again, and that time got a different response: tears. She was exhausted and burnt out. The game-playing had practically destroyed her. She left the industry altogether, had a wobbly year refocusing, then took up her other passion—food. Debbie now runs a small café and is blissfully happy. We've had several conversations over the years as to why she stuck it out so long, why she put up with the abuse, and it all came down to her resilience and upbringing. Debbie's father wasn't a particularly good man, let alone a good father, and after a few drinks, he was plain nasty. Debbie learnt from an early age to keep her head down and just put up with it. Being too resilient can mean you lose perspective on what you should and shouldn't put up with. It prevents you from pushing back or asking for help and support. It can have long term health consequences.

For me, I didn't realise the importance of checking in and listening to myself until a tsunami of stressors hit all at once. I'd divorced my husband, which meant I was on my own with two teenagers (who were done hanging around with Mum), hormones were messing with my head and piling weight on, and on top of that, I lost a big work contract due to the company firing thousands of employees. The final straw came from my attempt to get out of a financial trap in Sydney. A "friend" introduced me to an investment group; it seemed legitimate. An accountant was involved. The numbers added up, but to be safe, I diversified and invested in three investment schemes, not just one. I thought diversity would be sensible. Little did I know, all three investments would go belly-up and wipe hundreds of thousands of dollars out of my account.

Retrospectively, this was the lowest time of my life—lower than the loss of my mother. But in true Tracey style, I was determined to be okay over the next couple of months. I told myself, "You've got this. You'll be fine." I was still going out, celebrating people's birthdays, living a "normal" life, pretending to the world I was okay. I was still going to the gym despite being exhausted—no, beyond exhausted. I was a walking zombie.

It was only after a call from my private detective—yes, I hired my own private detective to try and track down one of the crooks I'd unwittingly invested in—that I found out he couldn't dig up anything on the man, let alone the money. It was gone; I was done. I couldn't face building my savings back up. I was done parenting; my teenagers didn't seem to need me anymore. I was done with relationships, marriage. No rose-tinted glasses there. I wasn't suicidal, but I couldn't see the point in living. Who for? What for?

When I finally crumbled in a heap and acknowledged I wasn't fine, life got bizarrely easier. I gave myself permission to not go out. Catching up with anyone but my inner circle was draining. I gave myself permission to not go to the gym. I've exercised all my life, but it was time to recuperate. Probably for the first time in my life, I admitted to my general practitioner, close friends, and teenagers I wasn't coping. I forgave myself. I forgave myself for the investments that went sour. I stopped beating myself up. I *finally* stopped beating myself up.

That compassion I showed myself was pivotal in my journey to finding joy again. I learned the importance of admitting to yourself that you need help, asking for help, and being open to receiving it. That was a major turning point in my life—I was finally able to treat myself the way I've treated others.

Treat *yourself* how you would treat others.

Admitting you're not coping is a strength, not a weakness. I see this so clearly now, and your recovery will be so much faster if you do. Being self-compassionate is all about mentally checking in with yourself, accepting where you're at, how you're feeling, listening to what you need, being kind to yourself, and learning to be a beautiful, non-judgemental friend to yourself.

In your busy life, try and regularly stop to have a real conversation with yourself. Acknowledge the reality of your life at the moment: the good, the bad, and the ugly. What do you need? Acknowledge how you're feeling. It's okay to feel sad, angry, scared, tired, pissed off, or lost. It's all okay!

When you come to terms with how you are really feeling and stop suppressing it, the tension from that emotion eases. This is simply part of the roller coaster ride of life. Even this phase will pass and give you hope. Be a precious friend to yourself. Be kind, not judgemental. As women, we are way too harsh on ourselves. Stop that harsh judgement and those unrealistic expectations. We are super women, not Superwoman. Instead, gently guide yourself through a series of baby steps towards a solution.

Always remain patient, kind, and non-judgemental towards yourself.

It is handy to remind ourselves that few people wear their hearts on their sleeves. Most of us have either been conditioned by parents or, more recently, social media to wear a happy mask all the time. This makes it very easy to feel like you're alone in a sticky situation. I guarantee you are *not* alone. At any given point in time, there will be many others in the same situation.

Consider this stressful situation: a dying parent. It is such a sad and challenging time. If you have a loving relationship with that parent, you won't want them to leave, and yet at the same time, you don't want their pain to continue. You wish they would die quickly and be out of their pain, then you feel guilty for having had such a thought and angry and sad you're even in this situation.

Conversely, even if you had a challenging relationship with your parent, you still don't want them to die, either. They are your parent. On a deeper level, you want to be able to resolve your issues and reconnect. Maybe you just want them to say, "I love you. I'm sorry. I'm proud of you." Any would be good, and *then* they can die. Uh, oh…did you just think that? Then the guilt kicks in. Or, maybe you just want them to die quickly. You're done with them and their drama. Oops. In whooshes the guilt again, coupled with the sadness you never had a parent you could value. In fact, as you think about it, that makes you angry! See? Either way, this situation will bring up a plethora of conflicting views and emotions, and they are all okay. All of these emotions need to be heard. Don't suppress them or pretend they don't exist. Accept them without judgement. Be kind to yourself; you are a wonderful woman.

All of this is normal.

Acknowledging how you feel and accepting, not judging it, will bring you peace. It's time to love yourself.

Exercise 2:

Put time into your diary every week—or day, if life is currently stressful—to stop and be a great listener and counsellor to yourself. Find a quiet space, and use a journal to capture your thoughts. Writing things down helps us be more objective. Explore your current situation, the highs and the lows. Acknowledge the stressors in your life. Put these into perspective while being kind and patient with yourself, and start the gentle process of guiding yourself towards finding peace with the situation.

3. The Hugger

Some of us are naturally more comfortable reaching out to hug those in distress. You may not be the type to take homemade meals around or feel it's your place to offer advice. However, you may be great at holding a distressed person's hand or giving them a hug. Please know by hugging and holding another human being, whether they're in pain or not, you are doing a wonderful, wonderful thing.

Both empirical and anecdotal studies have found that babies who are not hugged daily are significantly less happy, healthy, and nourished throughout their lives, even if food is abundant (Goleman 1998). In Western society, it was only when doctors noticed a difference in babies held daily by nurses that they began to see the importance of skin-to-skin contact. The result? With an increase in hugs, babies were happier, cried less, and ate better. Grown-ups need daily hugs, too, regardless of whether they are well or not. Wellness will return much sooner if you receive love through a kind hug from another person (Light 2005, 5-21).

Researchers have found our bodies release cortisol under stressful situations. Cortisol is a stress hormone designed to help you cope in fight-or-flight situations. Cortisol is only designed to be released in short doses. The problem for many of us is we spend too much time living in highly stressed states and constantly producing high levels of cortisol. It can lead to weight gain, thinning skin, and weakening muscles. It's not good for us, and it's important we get these high levels of cortisol back to normal quickly.

One great way to reduce this stress hormone is with a hug. Yes! A hug triggers the introduction of our body's own anti-stress hormone, oxytocin. Simply giving someone under stress a supportive embrace or even holding their hand is a powerful way to start the healing process (Light 2005, 5-21).

Exercise 3:

This is about getting more anti-stress hormones in you. Find people in your circle who give warm, caring hugs, and hang out with them more. Let them know how awesome their hugs are and how much you appreciate them, and they will be sure to give you more. Hey, if we can teach the people around us to be more in tune with our emotions, let's do it.

My son and daughter are great huggers. They hold you, and it feels like they are there for you and not in a hurry to leave. Beautiful. If there are no huggers available, self-compassion is lovely, too. Pause—and I mean *pause*—in your busy day to give yourself a hug as long and generous as you would for someone else in distress. Hold your elbows in an embrace, or simply hold your hands supportively together. Send yourself love and self-compassion. Let yourself know you have your own back.

A self-hug is the "compassionate selfie." Always remember you are worth it.

Practical Strategies

Practise *all three* of the self-compassion techniques over the coming days. Ideally, make time to do each one daily. Focus on being kind and non-judgemental to yourself. Make notes on how you feel. You are practicing new skills, so be patient. You will find lots of time for you. It's just going to take a couple of attempts before you really nail delegating, simplifying, and dumping your tasks.

Importantly, when you have been able to DSD something, calculate the time you have saved. Spend it on yourself *wisely*. Even if you only saved twenty minutes this week, this is twenty minutes for you. Don't waste it! Maybe sit on a park bench with a coffee. Put the timer on so you don't think about anything else, and embrace the beautiful world surrounding you. Look at the skyline, clouds, trees, buildings, colours, shapes, and people. Simply enjoy the fact you are there with the abundance that is all around you.

Delegating, Simplifying, and Dumping:
Techniques to Find More Time

Examine the example below, then apply these changes to your life both in or out of work. This example is based on a family of four with husband David and teenage children Josh and Tess.

Tasks I'm currently doing	Delegate, Simplify, or Dump?	To whom, how, and when?	Time saved per week
Shop at ALDI			
Clean bathroom	Delegate	Josh / weekly	20 mins
Clean kitchen	Delegate	Tess / weekly	20 mins
Buy present for Auntie Sue	Simplify	Online	40 mins
Cook dinner Sat.			
Cook dinner Sun.	Delegate	David	30 mins
Cook dinner Mon.			
Cook dinner Tue.	Delegate	Josh	30 mins
Cook dinner Wed.			

Cook dinner Thu.	Delegate	Tess	30 mins
Cook dinner Fri. (w/ guests)			
Make lunch Mon.			
Make lunch Tues.	Under family negotiation		
Make lunch Wed.			
Make lunch Thu.			
Make lunch Fri.	Under family negotiation		
Wash clothes Sat.			
Iron clothes Sat.	Dump ironing sheets		20 mins
Fold and put away clothes			
Change sheets Sun.			
Make beds			
Clean stove and microwave			

Empty kitchen bins			
Put bins out			
Dust			
Vacuum			
Pay bills			
Find a financial advisor			
Research holiday			
Book holiday			
Weed garden			
Mow lawn	Delegate	Student employee	40 mins
Cut hedges			
Bake birthday cake	Dump	Buy one	40 mins
Total minutes saved this week:		270 mins = 4 hours and 30 mins for you!	

In this exercise, you have saved yourself an amazing four and a half hours, even though you are still doing the lion's share of the housework. Now the question is, how will you use this time? Use it wisely on you.

Managing Time with Work Tasks

After you have combed through your work tasks and given them the DSD treatment, this next exercise will help prioritise your tasks, reduce time spent procrastinating, and aid you in not spending too long on tasks by being a perfectionist. All of this means more time for you, making it easier for you to leave work at a reasonable time.

First, list all the tasks you have to do and when they need to be completed. Estimate the time you think it will take to do these tasks. Highlight the tasks you feel are priorities to complete today so your day is successful. Block out time in your diary to carry out those tasks; this is your start and finish time for this task. In this case, you need to schedule four and a half hours today. Put in diary entries to cover this time, and don't let others overwrite these "meetings" you have with yourself. Make the same commitment to yourself as you would someone else. With the "Priorities for today" column, start with the one that you want to do least, get that done first, and then move on to the next least favourite…

Tasks	Completed by	Estimated time required	Priorities for today
Call unhappy client (resolve)	ASAP	30 mins	Resolve client issues (30 mins)

Performance review with Bill	ASAP	1 hr	Talk to Bill (1 hr)
Create report for marketing	17th	6 hrs	Start marketing (2 hrs)
Prepare board papers	18th	4 hrs	Start board papers (1 hr)
New draft targets for Q1	20th	3 hrs	
Expenses	30th	1 hr	
Organize get-together	No deadline	40 mins	
Total time to budget for this week:		4 hours and 30 minutes	

Note: Do tasks required to be done today first.

Importantly, you have only scheduled four and a half hours of work today, even though you are expected to work eight. This is because other things like meetings and conferences will no doubt come up. If you get into the habit of planning each day, you will be on track with your tasks, which will make you feel more in control and less overwhelmed. Plus, when you have completed your priorities for the day, you can leave work at a sensible time!

Chapter 2: Time to Get Realistic

Time for a reality check. This entire book was designed to help you become the woman you were always meant to be and find joy in your life again, along with more fun, energy, and time for yourself. To manifest all of this, we need to start off by being honest with ourselves.

Chapter one was all about self-compassion. We learned how to do the following for ourselves: find time; be a kind, supportive listener; give validation and have a greater understanding of why we feel the way we do; and recognize the first steps to changing our negative feelings. This chapter has two main takeaways. First, learning how to stop being our own worst enemy, and second, learning how to find even more time for ourselves.

How did it go delegating, simplifying, and dumping tasks at home and at work? How much time did you save?

When I work with clients one on one, they save an average of about four hours at work and four at home. That's *eight* hours a week carved out from their busy schedule and given back to them. Impressive! However, they don't create that time for themselves on the first pass. No, most come back saying they didn't have time to do the exercise. Oh, the irony.

If you read chapter one and moved on without doing the exercises, that's okay; just lock in some time to go back and do them. They are the foundation for finding more time for yourself. If you did do the exercises, well done.

Now, my instincts and experience tell me there will still be more tasks you can delegate, simplify, or dump, which is exciting. To help you create even more time in your busy week, I'd like to look at the potential "blockers" getting in the way of doing so.

Before we talk about your blockers, I want to talk about your brain, a far more interesting subject. Your brain operates in two parts. Bob Proctor and his "Thinking into Results" program gave the best explanation of this: it's all about your conscious and subconscious brain. Our conscious brain is the *knowing* part of our brain. It learns new things through the five senses. It is our connection to the world. Our conscious brain programs and feeds information to our subconscious brain, which is our automatic pilot. This is the part of the brain that guides us to *do* most things, and it greatly impacts our behaviour.

We spend most of our time doing things subconsciously. For example, do you actively think about the act of driving home from work? I bet you don't. I bet you're thinking about what to cook for dinner or that irritating email you received at work. Suddenly, you pull up in your driveway. Your brilliant subconscious brain, your automatic pilot, got you home.

The fact is, we spend most of our day—over 90 percent—operating on auto-pilot (Proctor 2014).] Our brain does this to be efficient. It's ingenious that the brain can program ways to behave so it doesn't have to use valuable "thinking energy" on everyday stuff.

Let's have a look at what you did this morning. I bet you got out of bed, went to the bathroom, and brushed your teeth, didn't you? You didn't consciously think about that. No, that would take too long and slow you down. Long ago, you locked in the belief that brushing your teeth is good dental hygiene, and you need to do it twice a day. That belief likely came from your parents, who told you night and day for years, "Brush your teeth." Now, the moment you walk into the bathroom and grab the toothbrush, your auto-pilot kicks in. Brain efficiency at its best.

We have hundreds, if not thousands of beliefs locked in like that, guiding us daily about how we should behave as well as the best route home from work. I, for example, have the belief it's rude to be late. This must have come from my mother; I can't be late if I try. I'm always one of the first people to arrive for dinner. I've arrived at a host's house right at seven o'clock as requested, and, to my surprise, they were still in the shower! My auto-pilot astounds me. I could have vomiting children, wardrobe malfunctions, and a distressed friend, and I would still arrive on time. Auto-pilots are powerful and should not be underestimated.

"How does this affect *me*?" I hear you ask. Well, your conscious brain will have read chapter one about making time and thought, Yes, that all makes sense. I can see how that works. But most of you won't have done much about it because of beliefs programmed into your subconscious brain. If you have the belief, *As a mother, I should cook and clean for everyone. It's my role,* then you will really struggle to delegate or simplify, let alone dump because that is how you have been conditioned since childhood. Even if you want to have more time, your conditioning and beliefs have programmed your subconscious brain about how to behave.

Laura, an old friend of mine from school, struggled with this. When she was married, she did most things around the house. No, I'm being too generous. She did *everything* around the house—a bit like my mother, except she had her husband, a fit and healthy man, living with her. He was lazy with a capital "L." Laura complained he never put his washing in the wash basket. Yes, out of everything, that's all she complained about! I suggested as a way to "train" him and reduce frustration to have a conversation along the lines of, "Okay, family (teenagers needed to be trained, too), only clothes placed in the wash basket will be washed."

I left Laura with this pearl of wisdom, thinking it made sense, and she'd do it. But at the time, I didn't realise the difference between our subconscious and conscious brain, nor did I understand her conditioning of what men and women do around the house. The next time I was home visiting my mum, I asked her how it went.

"Oh, you know," Laura said. "It seems like I'm being churlish not picking up a few things from the floor."

That was Laura's belief system at play. Consciously, she wanted more time to herself. She didn't feel it was fair that she did everything, but her subconscious brain believed she should, so she did.

We are all affected by this to a greater or lesser degree depending on the programming of our subconscious brain. We can intellectually say yes to an idea such as going on a diet or joining a gym, but if it doesn't fit with the belief system our subconscious brain operates by, we will still eat cake because our subconscious brain believes cake will relax us and make us feel better. We only turn up to the gym once because our subconscious brain believes we look awful in gym gear—or even worse, sweating—and besides, the gym is hard work and something to be avoided. Then, ironically, in our conscious brain, we will spend hours, days, or weeks beating ourselves up thinking we are useless and can't stick to a plan. Sound familiar?

The trick is to give our subconscious brain new beliefs to suit our lifestyle today. What we need to do is identify old beliefs and blockers, banish them, find new beliefs, and invite them in.

When you come across an old belief (which you will do in this chapter, chapter three, and chapter four), first write it out on a piece of paper, then write a new, more appropriate belief on a different piece of paper. Now, ceremoniously burn the old belief. Go on. Trust me; I know it seems illogical, but we aren't dealing with our logical, conscious brain. By burning the old belief, you are symbolically letting it go. Have reminders of the new belief around the house: on the mirror in your bathroom, on your computer, and wherever else you might spot it. Repeat it to yourself throughout the day until you have locked it into your subconscious mind. Here's an example:

Old belief: It's okay to have cake. No one sees me, and it makes me feel less stressed or bored.

New belief: I love snacking on healthy food and looking after my body.

As you are reprogramming your subconscious brain to this new belief, set yourself up for success. With the previous example, have lots of healthy food easily available throughout the week: carrots, celery, chopped nuts, and seeds. That way, when you enter the kitchen, it's easier to follow through with your goal. This will also help you avoid temptation. Be kind to yourself and *don't buy cake.* For the rest of the family, they can buy or bake cake themselves if they want it. Allow yourself to eat cake once a week, as a treat, away from your house. You might say, "I swim on Fridays, and my swim team sometimes shares a cake after our swim." I'm not saying you can't eat cake—just don't eat it on auto-pilot, which is what you have been doing.

Make sense?

Read the list below, and see which of these blockers or beliefs could be getting in the way of releasing yourself of tasks. It's okay to have more than one.

- If I delegate my tasks, I believe I won't be working hard enough. I must work hard to make a living.
- If I delegate that task, I believe they won't do it as well as me, and it has to be right.
- If I delegate that task, I believe they won't like me, love me, or they won't feel as loved.

- If I delegate that task, I believe they will be overloaded.
- If I dump that task, I believe it's a slippery slope and a sign I'm being lazy or worse, not coping.
- If I create time for myself, I believe I'll have to face myself. I prefer distraction.

Take a couple of deep breaths, and let's review this list. Think about these statements and reflect honestly about which of these may apply to you. Which statement(s) really resonate with you? Not the ones you *think* should resonate, but the ones that really, really do.

The quicker you understand and accept the blockers that have been getting in the way of freeing you up all these years, the better.

Once you've identified the key statement(s) that resonate with you, let's look at them in a self-compassionate light and see if we can adjust your perspective.

Blocker: If I delegate my tasks, I believe I won't be working hard enough. I must work hard to make a living.

I see this one a lot in the corporate world. The workload can be huge, and long hours can be seen as a badge of honour. They're not, by the way. But because so many people operate from their sub-conscious belief they should work hard to make a living, they've equated work with "working hard." Their working life becomes "hard" mainly by taking on more and more tasks and spending longer and longer hours in the office, which is why they end up feeling like a hamster on a wheel they can never get off.

It is absolutely critical you understand, recognise, and accept we are talking about *your* life. You are the boss, leader, director, CEO, CFO, and managing director of *your* life. It's up to you to decide whether your work should be hard or joyful, and it's up to *you* to decide how much time you spend working each week. My uncle John was a veterinarian, and I visited him once to see a cat that had just had kittens. I was about twelve years old, and these funny little creatures with eyes still shut enthralled me. We must've spent hours talking about his work. It struck me then, even as a twelve-year-old, that he loved his work. In fact, it wasn't work to him at all; it was his passion, his hobby, something he loved to do. Work doesn't have to be hard unless you believe it should. Even if you love your work, like my uncle John, it's okay to leave work at a sensible time. It's okay to have a lunch break. In fact, it's more than okay—it's vital. We all need time to recharge our internal batteries. Recharging them is what gives us the space, patience, and energy to give to others. My clients often talk about trying to find a work-life balance, as if it's some kind of mystic art. It's not mystical or a specialised art form—just less work!

You need this time to listen to your heart and instincts. You don't have to do everything, and you don't have to do everything today. Taking time out from work to recharge your batteries needs to be done daily. My suggestions would be to have an afternoon nap, leisurely bath, get a massage, take a walk in the park, or simply lie on the sofa and read a book. Learn the art of relaxing. What you do with your extra time is your choice. Choose wisely.

Possible mantras for you:

"I don't have to work hard to be successful."

"Saying no frees me up to say yes to things I want to do."

"I am the CEO of my life, and I make great decisions for myself."

"I love having time to spend on me."

Action: burn the old belief, and have reminders of your new belief everywhere.

In the workplace, the other aspect to consider is managing the perception of how you are seen at work. I often tell women there are two roles they need to carry out at work. The first role is to be great at whatever they are paid to do. The second role is to manage the perception of being great at what they do. The latter is a skill many women don't realise they need. They get promoted because people perceive they are great at their job, so manage that perception in such a way they don't have to work long hours, and no one would dream of giving them more work because everyone knows they are already busy doing a great job.

Blocker: If I delegate that task, I believe they won't do it as well as me, and it has to be right.

Ah, the joys of perfectionism. Actually, I want to be very real here; there is *no* joy in being a perfectionist. It's a tough trait to have. It is a high stressor that can lead to anxiety and depression.

If this is a trait you admire and cherish in yourself, yes, you might produce great work in the eyes of others, but the toll on yourself and your family can be extreme. Let's gauge exactly where you are on the perfectionism meter.

Circle the answer most appropriate to you in the following questions. Be honest. Go with your first instinct.

1. When you've finished a task, which do you do?

    a. Look back and feel pleased with what I've done.

    b. Notice the mistakes.

    c. Put it completely out of my mind.

2. Is procrastination a problem for you?

    a. No, I just dive into stuff.

    b. Yes, I worry it be done correctly because it's important.

    c. Yes, because I get distracted by other things.

3. When you look at the work of others, which do you do?

    a. Marvel at what they've achieved.

    b. Notice their mistakes.

    c. I don't really look at the work of others; life is too short.

4. Would you say you are difficult to please?

    a. Not particularly. People say I'm relaxed.

    b. Yes, they would say I have rather high standards.

    c. Sometimes; I like to help people be the best they can

be.

5. How do you feel when things fail?

    a. I don't think about it much.

    b. I hate it; I will relive it in my head and beat myself up for it.

    c. I hate it, but understand it's an opportunity to learn.

6. How do you feel if someone offers you constructive criticism?

    a. I don't pay much attention to it. I'm pretty self-aware.

    b. I can't stand it. It feels like an attack.

    c. Providing they phrase it properly, it's another opportunity to learn.

You have probably noticed all "B's" deal with perfectionism.

If you chose mostly "A's" or "C's," perfectionism isn't a trait that gets in the way of simplifying your life. Move on, and see if any of the other blockers below resonate.

If most of your answers were "B's," perfectionism is a strong trait for you. At this point, you'll either be saying, "Oh, no! How am I ever going to change this?" or "Yeah, and your point is? There's nothing wrong with being a perfectionist."

Let's be clear—there's nothing wrong with doing a job well. There is, however, a lot wrong with becoming so obsessed with doing a job perfectly it takes time away from you and others. It is also not healthy to procrastinate and waste time because you set such high standards for yourself you don't know where to begin. So, if you've scored mostly "B's" and have just outed yourself as a perfectionist, firstly, accept this is who you are at the moment. Secondly—and this is the important one—letting go of this trait is paramount in being able to get your life onto a more relaxed and stress-free track, enabling you to stop and smell the roses.

You may not have realised it, but your perfectionism has been getting in the way of your thriving. It is likely at this stage of life, you already have a load of responsibilities on your plate, and it is vital you release some of the pressures so you can thrive once more. Your perfectionistic high standards are getting in the way of delegating, simplifying, or dumping and thus really being able to engage in your own pursuits. These DSD skills are ones you need to focus on developing very carefully. If not, you'll be stuck in a grumpy loop, and that's not what we're about. We're all about helping you thrive again.

As part of your self-compassion journey, set yourself a goal to ease up on your high standards and allow yourself to take the pressure off. Perfectionists often struggle with procrastination; since they set themselves such high standards, this can create a fear of starting at all. Set times to start and finish a task. Identify what "good enough" looks like so you know when you are finished. Use mantras such as, "Good enough is good enough." Stick notes with this mantra up on your fridge, bathroom mirror, computer, and car. Remind yourself daily, "Good enough really is good enough."

Here's an example of a goal to help ease up your perfectionism:

Old version: Write a marketing plan for new product XYZ. (The challenge with this goal is there are no typical standards. This means you can allow yourself way too many hours to pore over this task, creating a document so thick and detailed no one will actually read, and sadly, no one will spot the talented ideas within.)

New version: Submit a *draft* marketing plan for new product XYZ for team discussion by the twenty-third of March. Commence working on the plan on Wednesday the seventeenth in the afternoon (with time allocated in your diary). Use the existing marketing plan for ABC product as a template, and with any uncertain areas, either ask immediately for feedback from Tim, your boss, or leave blank for the team to come up with ideas.

The aim of this goal by saying "draft" is to remind you it doesn't have to be perfect.

Whatever you submit, the team will have their own views on, and a draft will be an ideal starting point for discussion. Besides, you'll be less likely to get cranky with the changes they request when it's in draft form. Setting deadlines to start and finish will help avoid procrastination and limit over-working. It's okay to ask others for assistance. This will reduce your self-imposed pressure, and that will speed up your delivery in turn.

If you allow yourself to ease up on your standards, it will help simplify your tasks and delegate superfluous tasks to others.

Without those crippling high standards, others will be more willing to take on more of your tasks.

Another aspect to consider is the impact your perfectionism is having on others. Others may want to do some of these tasks for you to help you. They may see you as overloaded. They may be worried about you, want you to trust them more, want more responsibility, to feel more empowered, more opportunities to grow, and you know what? By not delegating, you are stifling them at every juncture. Not cool. Perfectionists are masters at teaching those around them to be helpless. If you continually rehang or refold the washing family members have just hung or folded, they will stop trying to help you in the first place.

The time has come for you to review your task list again. Phone a friend if this seems scary or if you want an impartial opinion. Work out the following:

- Which tasks can be delegated and to whom?
- Which can be simplified and how?
- Which can be dumped altogether?

Possible mantras for you:

"Good enough is great for me."

"I'm striving for progress, not perfectionism."

"I choose connection over perfection."

"I'm perfectly imperfect."

Action: burn the old belief, and have reminders of your new belief everywhere.

Okay, back to other potential blockers getting in the way of DSD.

Blocker: If I delegate that task, I believe they won't like me, love me, or they won't feel as loved.

This blocker is linked to the belief that doing things for others is a way of showing love. There is nothing inherently wrong with this belief until our subconscious takes it to extremes. *If I don't do everything for others, it's a sign I don't love them,* or *If I don't do everything for my partner or child, I'm a bad partner or mother,* or *If I don't do everything for my partner or child, they won't love me.* As you read, I know you'll think, *That's ridiculous; I shouldn't have to do everything!* Great, now that you've accepted you don't have to do everything, let's explore this blocker that tends to appear more in tight-knit relationships. Which tasks can you delegate, simplify, or dump? So much comes down to the conversation you have around the task. Let's look at cooking, a task that, as you may have gathered, is not dear to my heart, and I'm very happy to delegate.

If I suggest to the family they each cook once a week and I cook the rest, does that sound fair? Yes, it does. It also means instead of cooking seven times a week (considering just the evening meal), you are down to four times a week, assuming it's a family of four with two children who are able to safely cook on their own. By the way, my children have been cooking since they were ten years old, and the delightful consequence is now, as teenagers, they are more than capable cooks. In fact, my daughter has gone on to study cookery. She has become so natural in the kitchen, and it appears we have tapped into an amazing talent.

Did my family like it in the beginning when I suggested they cook? Of course not. Did they see it as reasonable? Yes, they did. I was still doing the lion's share of the cooking, but I managed to wangle myself out of cooking three dinners a week, and to me, that was worth more than all the gold in the Grand Bazaar in Istanbul.

Sometimes, people have to learn to suck up responsibility. You may need to teach them how to accept it, but once done, you *must* give that responsibility over. That includes working out what to cook and how to cook it. Go for a walk when others are cooking or lock yourself in the bathroom, or they will ask endless questions: What shall I cook? How do I...? Where is...? These questions will drive you nuts, and you may eventually cave in and cook it yourself! *Not* the outcome we are looking for.

If you are carrying out the task as an expression of love, it can be a beautiful gesture. Doing for others is classed as one of the love languages in Gary Chapman's book, *The 5 Love Languages: The Secret to Love that Lasts.* Let's look at the reality:

- Is your effort seen as love? (If not, delegate, simplify, dump.)
- Is it appreciated? (If not, delegate, simplify, dump.)

- Is it reciprocated? (If not, delegate, simplify, dump.)
- Are you being taken for granted? (If yes, delegate, simplify, dump.)
- You are a mother, wife, employee, or boss—not a servant.

Possible mantras for you:
"I love empowering others to learn new skills."
"I'm a wonderful partner or mother, not a servant."
"I respect and love myself and know when to stop over-caring."

Action: burn the old belief, and have reminders of your new belief everywhere.

Do something today your future self will love.

Blocker: If I delegate that task, I believe they will be overloaded.

I often see this one in the workplace with caring managers and leaders who are reluctant to delegate additional work to the team because they will possibly get overwhelmed. There are many challenges with this thought process. Firstly, the team is often desperate to have work delegated to them so they can develop new skills. They see their manager is overloaded, and that causes frustration because they care, too. When extra work doesn't come their way, they create their own belief their manager doesn't trust them to do the work properly, which starts to erode their relationship. To avoid these misunderstandings, have a conversation with the intended delegate and find out where they're at. Get them to delegate, simplify, or dump some of their tasks in order to take on your higher responsibility ones.

Remember:

- Being lazy isn't an excuse for others not to help you.
- Just because you are a woman does not mean you should do all the housework, especially if you are also working.
- If you have children, you are their mother, not servant.
- If you work and don't have children, it doesn't mean you should stay later at work because others need to pick their kids up from school. Have some evening commitments that force you to leave the office. Learn how to rock climb, go dancing, or have dinner with a friend.
- Holding onto tasks instead of delegating gets in the way of being promoted.
- Holding onto tasks instead of delegating to others gets in the way of their development.

Possible mantras for you:
"I am great at empowering others."
"I am great at helping others learn."
"I am a master delegator."

Action: burn the old belief, and have reminders of your new belief everywhere.

Blocker: If I dump that task, I believe it's a slippery slope and a sign I'm being lazy or worse, not coping.

This relates to how you see yourself, your worthiness, self-compassion, self-care, and ability to recognise downtime. These are valuable—in fact, *crucial*—for you. As corny as the saying is, "We have one life. It's a journey that should be savoured," it's true. Giving yourself space to breathe and time to relax is all part of the journey of being kind to yourself. Consider how you would counsel an overwhelmed friend, someone frazzled with life. What would you say to her if she could create more free time for herself?

"Take it," I hear you say. "Enjoy every second. You deserve it. You've worked so hard and cared for everyone; it's *your* turn. You are worthy of time off."

These are the self-compassion messages you need to say to yourself. Pick the one that resonates most for you or write your own, and stick it up where you can see it often: mirror, fridge, computer, etc. Now review your task list, and let's start delegating, simplifying, and dumping *properly*. Savour the beautiful time you have created for yourself.

Possible mantras for you:

"I'm investing time in myself."

"I'm giving myself time to stop and smell the roses."

"I like spending time with myself."

Action: burn the old belief, and have reminders of your new belief everywhere.

The difference between successful people and really successful people is that really successful people say no to almost everything.
–Warren Buffett

Blocker: If I create time for myself, I believe I'll have to face myself. I prefer distraction.

This is a tricky blocker. It's actually about avoidance, and the very nature of this blocker means we avoid admitting we have it. To avoid the pain of past conflict, abandonment, and basically all the lousy stuff that hasn't been properly acknowledged or dealt with, we keep ourselves busy. We take on projects, renovate, work longer hours, care for others, run around plumping cushions to remove bits of fluff that aren't even there.

I call this the "I'm fine" state. You're not *fine.* You are an overly resilient woman who needs to stop and connect with herself. When we were younger, keeping ourselves busy may have been a survival mechanism; we didn't have to consider the things going on around us if we were busy. At the time, it seemed like a great coping mechanism, and it may well have been, but that's all it was—a coping mechanism to help survive, not thrive. Later in life, this hectic avoidance of spending time with yourself is keeping you manically busy, and it's exhausting. Pushing away your past feelings is not self-compassionate. You need to face the pain and validate your suffering to be able to find closure and move on.

This is the hardest blocker to break. We can be in denial so much it blinds us, but removing it will give greater harmony to yourself, and that is joyous.

Possible mantras for you:

"I love the real me."

"Vulnerability is the birthplace of innovation, creativity, and change." –Brene Brown

"You either walk inside your own story and own it, or you stand outside your story and hustle for your worthiness." – Brene Brown

Action: burn the old belief, and have reminders of your new belief everywhere.

Reprogramming your subconscious brain is all about replacing no longer useful beliefs with more appropriate ones for today. This process will take several weeks. Have reminders everywhere of your new belief. Say it out loud. Smile when you say it; this is the start of the new, improved you. Then, with this new belief locked in, review your task list. Delegate, simplify, and dump. Get someone to guide you if needed. Savour any free time you have created. Use it wisely.

Chapter 3: Smash Your Conditioning

I want to talk to you about burnt chops. Yes! Burnt chops. This concept was introduced to me by a beautiful woman from the Country Women's Association when I was visiting Orange, a city in Central New South Wales.

The concept is, when sharing a plate of food with family or friends, you reserve any burnt chops for yourself. All the good stuff you give to others, and you only accept the dregs, leftovers, the worst of the lot.

This is a concept I've been familiar with all my life. As with many of us, it was part of my conditioning from childhood. If a guest came over, they would be served first, then the men, children, and last of all, my mother. She always got the burnt chop. It was always someone else who got the chocolate finger on top of the cake or perfect lasagne portion from the pan.

It was a long drive back to Sydney, and the "burnt chop" analogy weighed heavily on my mind. At the time, I was married and had primary school children. It could be said that with my cooking, we all got a lot of burnt chops, but in reality, I always got the dodgy plate. I realised I had taken on too much of my mother's "generosity of spirit" and given everyone else the best bits—not just of my food, but of my life.

It has taken a while, but I've realised I have a duty to care for myself. Now, I make sure I share out the best plates at home to include *myself.* When it's my turn, I feel special. It's funny; I can't explain it, but seeing my perfect, not dodgy plate feels gorgeous! I'm recognising my worthiness, and it makes me feel warm inside. It brings a smile to my face. It's bizarre how a simple plate of food can make you feel worthy.

This social conditioning at home when growing up can play a big part in who we are today. The more we understand and accept our past conditioning, the better we can choose which parts help or hinder us in our present.

It is this past conditioning that has programmed your subconscious brain—your auto-pilot. This auto-pilot controls how you behave and interact with people and surroundings. If we can identify which conditioning is a hindrance and needs to be released from our lives, it will free us up to change our subconscious program and become the women we were always meant to be.

If you look back at your childhood and think, *It was pretty good,* then I'm delighted. For a large part, so was mine. Regardless, conditioning is still at play, both in the home or at school. Some of it will have served you well, and some may continue to hinder you. It's time to release these negative conditionings.

Exercise:

For this exercise, dedicate some time to reflect and make notes. When you have gone as far as you can, pause, and revisit it the next day. See what you can add. If you have a close sibling or extended family, you may want to get their input to jog your memory.

Tackle this task with compassion, kindness, and love. It is not about judging your parents; they were doing the best they could. This is about *you*, understanding your conditioning, and deciding which parts are helpful and which are a hindrance. Think about your childhood and consider how you were told to behave.

- What did your mother often say to you?
- How did your father speak with or to you?
- Was it different from what your mother said?
- Did your father say different things to your brother or sister than to you?
- Who else commented on your behaviour or told you how to behave: grandparents, school, religious institutes?

Here are some examples I can recall growing up. It is not an exhaustive list, but it may get you started:

"Play nicely."

"Who do you think you are? Don't get above yourself."

"Girls should be seen and not heard."

"Share your toys."

"Give someone else a turn," or "Wait your turn."

"Play quietly."

"Don't interrupt."

"If you don't have anything nice to say, don't say it."

"That's not very ladylike," in response to arguing back or not sitting up straight.

"You're being hysterical," in response to objecting to a situation.

"No, you can't go out on your own. It's not safe for girls."

"Girls can't..." (fill in the blank). When I was still in school, I wanted to be an airline pilot or captain of a ship. Instead, I was encouraged to either become a nurse or a bank teller.

"Don't talk to strangers."

"Anger is bad and unladylike."

"It's unladylike to talk about money."

"Just mime the words," in response to my singing, from a teacher.

"You're just not very bright, are you?"

"Don't argue; it's rude."

"Just tell your friends your mum and dad got divorced."

"Don't go out with wet hair; you'll catch a cold."

"Remember your manners."

"Think of the starving..." (Fill in a struggling country.)

"What will the neighbours say?"

"It's rude to be late."

Looking at my list, there are some I understand and even use with my children. Manners are important to me. Listening in a conversation and waiting your turn is vital in having balanced conversation. I appreciate the value of being kind and giving to others, but not at the expense of yourself, especially when you have little to give.

What I notice with my childhood list is the common theme of putting everyone else first. I was very firmly last. Everyone else's playtime with toys and their point of view seemed to be considered more important than mine.

My list makes me realise, quite simply, I was never encouraged to put myself first, express my views, or be heard, and clearly no one expected me to amount to much academically.

Understand how this conditioning has cemented beliefs within you. With this exercise, we can get bogged down in emotion, grief from our childhood, sadness of wasted years, or anger at our parents. I have a letter-writing technique for you to assist in releasing this emotion. But for this exercise, try and be curious, like a detective putting the pieces together.

An example to get you started: from my conditioning, I formed the belief I wasn't very bright. Therefore, it shaped the way I behaved, and I continually felt the need to prove I was smart to people. I'm certain I chose a civil engineering degree to prove this point, mainly to my absent father, an architect. My subconscious belief was, *Maybe if I have a civil engineering degree, he'll see how bright I am and love me.* Which, of course, was flawed logic, and he didn't.

Old conditioning: I'm not very bright.

New conditioning: I'm an intelligent woman who listens to my intuition for guidance.

Repeat this daily, and have reminders throughout your life.

Evaluate your childhood conditioning and consider the impact these seemingly throw-away statements have had on your life. Work out how this conditioning has formed beliefs within you. Keep and embrace those which are helpful, and continue to practice them. Release the unhelpful ones by burning and replacing them with a new belief to start the process of reprogramming your subconscious brain.

When you have identified the statements that no longer apply to you, enjoy the behaviours you have now freed yourself up to do. For example, if you no longer care about what others think, what would you like to do? Dye your hair pink? Buy outrageous underwear? Chat with strangers at the bus stop? Take the biggest piece of cake? Be honest with people about how you really feel? Set these as actions to take in the coming weeks, and marvel at the new, improved you.

These days, I am putting myself first more often. I placate less and express my views regularly. It's a delicious feeling. Have I become selfish? No, I don't think I have; I still see myself as caring. I just have *my* needs in the picture now. Have I ruffled a few feathers along the way? Possibly. This is a new me. I'm less accommodating, and people have to adapt. I have changed for the better, I believe. Any change within yourself will change the dynamic of the relationships you are in, and you need to give others time to adjust. Most people will adapt and accept changes quickly, but for those who don't, maybe they aren't as healthy for you as previously thought. This is something we will explore further in Chapter 5: Oxygen Suckers, Get Out!

Oh, and don't forget, when you have released the ineffective conditioning and beliefs, review your tasks and see what you can further delegate, simplify, or dump. There has to be more.

Everything you believe is true. Challenge your reality by challenging your beliefs.

Letter to a parent or caregiver:

For those of you who reflected on your childhood and realised how magnificent your parents were, writing them a letter of thanks, even if they have passed, is a beautiful exercise. If you are blessed to have parents still alive, let them hear your appreciation in person. Saying thank you is a wonderful gift.

For some, reflecting on what parents did or didn't say or do can be very confrontational. If you have never faced this, you may need further support. I recommend reaching out to a wise friend or professional who can guide you in completing this exercise.

Importantly, go towards whatever emotion arises: anger, sadness, frustration, or fear. Acknowledge its existence. Living in denial may seem like a perfect survival methodology, but it will get in the way of truly thriving. It can cause discomfort within our bodies, like a car with a dirty engine; no matter how much you polish the outside, it's only a matter of time before it breaks down on you. Few of us have perfect childhoods, and besides which, what does that even mean? All of us have lessons to learn in order to grow, and part of that learning is accepting the reality of our past before releasing it and moving forward.

I found letter writing to be a great technique. As I mentioned before, I had no relationship with my father when I was growing up. Even when I was older and tried to reconnect, he showed no interest. It was the opposite of TV shows where families are happily reunited. The three instances my father and I met in person all consisted of awkward silences, inconsistences, and lies. I didn't get any hugs or love. Years later, to deal with the anger and sadness I was still clearly hanging onto, a counsellor guided me to write a letter to him, even though I suspected he had died many years before. I was guided to take my time with the letter, add to it daily, and keep going until I felt nothing more needed to be added. Then I was to ceremoniously release the letter to the universe by burning it or dissolving it in the sea.

I did. I started writing neatly, politely, as per my kind conditioning. I was very much in my head, not my heart. I addressed it, "Dear Dad." I didn't feel connected to the words; it felt mechanical, so I put my pen down and left it for the day.

The next day, I looked at what I had written and thought, "What bollocks!" I scratched out "Dear Dad" and wrote "Ken." I then went on a rant, and writing turned to scrawl. It was large, passionate, misspelt, and it felt right. I wrote until I ran out of words and tears. I breathed deeply and closed the book for the day.

The following day was interesting. As I read the pages, I didn't connect with the anger in the same way I had the previous day. I picked up the pen and started the conversation again. I wrote down the story as I saw it from his eyes, starting from just before my conception. As I wrote that story to Ken, part of me wanted to be angry, but I had an overwhelming sense of sorrow for him. In a relationship that had started out as a bit of fun, life had become complicated as I was about to enter the scene. I wasn't part of the plan. As I wrote, I started to understand there were no easy answers for Ken, and that whichever direction he went in, it would cause someone pain.

The next time I took up my pen, my writing took Ken through my childhood and adulthood. I told him about my children. I felt sad for what he had missed out on. I shared my business ideas, and it was then I had a real "Aha!" moment. I admit I don't know much about him even to this day. I know he wasn't as bad as I had believed as a child, and when I think of him now, I recognize his sharp business mentality, healthy sense of self-preservation, and I feel he rarely gave a hoot about what other people thought. All that time I had denied being anything like my father, but I realised I actually needed more of my father's traits to balance out the over-giving nature of my mother. These days, I find myself tapping into my father's energy during quiet moments. Without any expectations of warmth or love, I consider what his approach and advice would be. I sometimes sense a brutal encouragement from him. "Stop messing around, and get on with it." In a funny way, it makes me smile. I let him know I forgave him, and I let go of a lot of pain.

This letter is to help you move forward. I don't recommend sending this letter unless it's a beautiful note of thanks.

Holding on to anger or resentment is like holding on to a burning coal and expecting the other person to feel pain. Forgive them, release yourself from the pain, and let it go.

–Buddha

As a side note, when my book was about to go to print, my intuition bizarrely told me to write a letter to my grandparents. I had always felt they had been a bit harsh with my mother, but I felt it was time to let go of my stories and forgive them, even though they passed decades ago. What fascinated me was, by writing the letter, I ended up apologising to them for feeling that way. Writing the letter gave me clarity. I saw their point of view much more clearly, and it totally changed my opinion. I asked them for forgiveness, and I know—being the grandparents they were—their spirits forgave me with a wry smile, thinking, *She took her time, didn't she?*

If you feel guilty about something you have said or done, it's time you wrote to and forgave yourself. Otherwise, you will continue to feel the pain of that burning coal you are holding onto.

Chapter 4: Muzzle Your Inner Bitch

This has to be one of my favourite chapters. Get this right, and your life will be much less stressful!

Before you start this chapter, have you written some letters and released those deep feelings of anger, grief, frustration, hatred, and sadness? Have you reached a point of forgiveness and let go? Have you forgiven yourself? This is so important. We all do stupid things and misjudge situations. Forgive yourself. You, too, are worthy of forgiveness.

Now, onto muzzling our inner bitches. We talk to ourselves thousands of times a day. We have an inner conversation with ourselves from the moment we wake up to the time we fall asleep. Some of this inner chatter is useful: *Did I turn the iron off? I need to pick up tomatoes,* or *I'll go to the gym on the way home.*

But sadly, most of our self-talk is toxic; it damages our health, sabotages our self-worth, and ruins our self-esteem. This inner monologue is based on years and years of practise. We are masters at it, and we don't even realise we are doing it. Our self-talk is our own secret thing. It's running all the time in public places, private places, when we're trying to sleep, or when we are meant to be having fun. It's exhausting, and we are so used to hearing it, we actually believe it. This means our self-talk not only changes what we believe but the way we behave, hence how the world views us. The results we get in life are all ultimately from seemingly innocent, internal conversations.

For example, if every time I looked in the mirror I thought, *I'm fat. I'm old. I've got nothing to offer,* I'm going to lock that belief into my subconscious brain. Did you know there is no fact-checking by our subconscious brain? It believes whatever we program it to. With the belief, *I'm fat, old, and have nothing to offer* now firmly locked in, it affects how I behave every day. I won't go out as much. If I do go out socially, I will likely hang at the back of a crowd and wear clothes that camouflage the "weight" in neutral tones to make me blend into the background. The result is, I won't be included in as many conversations and will feel more isolated, which reinforces the belief *I'm fat, old, and have nothing to offer.* Our self-talk has a compound effect that typically brings us down, which is why I call our inner chatter, or self-talk, our "Inner Bitch." She's vicious, and she needs a muzzle.

Step 1: Acknowledge her existence.

Like any problem-solving exercise, the first and most powerful step is to acknowledge the problem. In this case, it's to accept that your self-talk is regularly feeding you lies and being really mean. She's just like that toxic school "friend" you hung around with on the playground, the one always in your ear, putting you down, challenging your thoughts, and making you feel bad.

Reading this may have stirred your own Inner Bitch. She is probably already in conversation with you, telling you she isn't a bitch—how ridiculous! As far as she is concerned, her only motive is to help you, and besides which, you do need to lose a few kilos.

Before your Inner Bitch gets carried away, let's explore this exercise. All you need is a small notebook and pen or the ability to take notes on your phone. It needs to be discreet enough you can carry it around each day to all the different settings you go to: work, social gatherings, family gatherings, shopping, gym, etc. You only need to do this for a couple of days.

When your Inner Bitch pipes up, jot down what she has to say in your notepad or record it on your phone. Attempt to capture the gist of all her statements. Believe me, we don't need them word for word.

Approach this exercise with curiosity. Think of yourself as a detective researching the typical statements your Inner Bitch comes up with. Avoid beating yourself up or telling yourself you are crazy—far from it; you are a very, very, normal woman.

Ideally, when you are over the shock of what you have

repeatedly been telling yourself after only the first day, I want you to start bringing humour in. Start laughing at yourself and your ridiculous unfounded statements that have formed beliefs in your subconscious brain. I can tell you right now not even having heard your Inner Bitch, she is lying, exaggerating, being unreasonable, and downright nasty. Check out these statements my clients had to put up with from their Inner Bitches.

- "I'm not qualified." (Ten years of experience and a PhD)
- "I'm too old." (Thirty-eight years old)
- "My son doesn't love me." (Three-year-old having a temper tantrum)

To help understand why our Inner Bitches are so vicious, it's useful to dig deeper to understand our brain's motivation.

Our brain's main focus is survival. It's about keeping us alive, not fulfilled, successful, or happy. Nope, just alive. In evolutionary terms, our brain hasn't had much time to evolve from our cave-dwelling days, and it still operates as if we are in that time. Our ancestors were always on the move, keeping themselves safe, and searching for food which was often in scarce supply. Even today, our primitive brains still operate with the same approach: looking out for danger, ways to conserve energy, and how to easily obtain food. If there is a choice between taking the stairs or using the escalator, your primitive brain will choose the escalator every time to conserve precious energy. It has no idea you have a desk job, sit all day, and really need some exercise. If you happen to be up at midnight and open the refrigerator, don't be surprised if your primitive brain goes in for a snack or two. Remember, our brain's innate survival drive is locked deep inside, it doesn't know when it will find food next, and it certainly has no idea you are going out for breakfast in the morning (Lieberman 2015).

Keeping ourselves safe is the highest priority for our rudimentary brain, and as a result, our brain is always on high alert for bad news, negative information, and life-threatening scenarios that could kill us. For our ancestors, these scenarios would have been: which marauding tribe might attack us? Which berries are poisonous? What does a sabre-toothed tiger look like before it attacks? To keep us alive, our primordial brain seeks out and hears negative over positive news, and it hardly needs any repetition for us to lock this information in as belief. Let's face it—if we didn't lock this negative information in, we could be killed the very next day if it meant life and death survival.

This is how our self-talk started out: keeping you safe, trying to protect you, and being on the lookout for all the "bad" in the world. When we were little, our self-talk may have kept us out of mischief and danger. It might've been highly useful, but now our self-talk has got her own sense of importance, and it is constantly misinterpreting and distorting our world.

Imagine your friend Janice is having a birthday party, and you're there to help celebrate. She's a lot older than you, but age has never gotten in the way of your friendship. Over the course of the evening, you get several lovely compliments on your outfit and hair until you meet one man who innocently asks, "Did you go to school with Janice?" Your self-talk (who is on the lookout for the bad), interprets this as he thinks you're the same age as Janice, and you further interpret this as, *He thinks I look old.* It is this *one* comment, this *one* piece of bad news you will fester on for days, if not months. All other gorgeous, positive compliments are overlooked. Instead, your self-talk will mull this I *look old* statement over and over again in your head. Boom! Your self-talk has suddenly locked a new belief into your subconscious brain—*I look old!*

Can you see how normal and easy it is for our self-talk to turn into an Inner Bitch? It's not really her fault; she was just born in the wrong era. But irrespective of her intentions to protect you, she is actually harming you, and it's time for her to go.

The process of capturing your self-talk and seeing the harshness of these daily comments can be very confrontational to start with. We have had this self-talk in our heads for years; we have accepted it without realising we don't need to. This is why so many of us choose to distract ourselves with excessive work, other people's problems, tidying, cleaning, exercise, alcohol, and medication. Please understand this is normal; you aren't alone. Be patient. Once you have reined in your negative self-talk, your Inner Bitch, your life will be filled with much more peace and harmony.

After three or four days have gone by and your notepad is full of self-talk statements, avoid beating yourself up with the harshness of it all, simply accept this is what you have been telling yourself for years—literally, years—and be ready to move on to some new positive self-talk.

It is confrontational when you see it written. With many women I have coached over the years undertaking this exercise, I ask what would happen if they gave this type of feedback to family members or co-workers. Tears often well up, accompanied by statements such as, "I'd be sacked!" "They would be devastated," "They'd hate me," or "They'd wonder why I was being so mean." Whatever the interpretation from this exercise, what *is* clear is when we capture our self-talk, we can display how excessively nasty we've been towards ourselves.

If you completed the above exercise, you will have realised your Inner Bitch is very much alive, well, and not doing you any favours. It's time to muzzle her. To support you, I'm giving a smorgasbord of techniques. "Who's speaking?" is a must for you. It's super powerful. Then, have a look at the other techniques and start implementing the one that resonates with you the most. Like any new skill, it requires practise and patience. They all work; they just need a bit of time and effort. But they are well worth it.

Step 2: Who's speaking?

A really powerful technique I have used with myself and with clients over the years is naming our self-talk. Naming it helps separate ourselves from our Inner Bitch. The more we separate ourselves from her, the happier we will be.

I get clients to give their self-talk a name that encapsulates its toxic nature. Mine is called "Nasty Nan." My mother had an elderly aunt called Nan, and my selfless, beautiful mum would often visit her to help around the house. Nan was the epitome of negativity, and I hated going. She complained about everything from the weather (too hot, too cold, too wet, too dry) to supermarkets, neighbours, television shows, and politics. She had an uncanny knack of picking fault with everyone she met and making you feel awkward and incompetent, even when you had gone out of your way to help. Nasty Nan is the perfect name for my self-talk. It reminds me my self-talk is unfounded, downright mean, and not worthy of attention.

Choose a name for your self-talk that resonates with you.

When you have found the perfect name for your self-talk, start to notice when she is speaking. You'll notice her more as you practise this technique. The first time you capture her in full flow, it is really satisfying and something to be celebrated. It's like you are finally on to her. You get the game she has been playing all these years, and it's time to stop her in her tracks.

Let me show you how to practically apply this knowledge. Imagine an idea has been presented to you for a business opportunity. You have been wanting to run your own business for years, and now could be just the right time. After the meeting, you drive home. You are so excited by this opportunity; this is the big break you have been looking for. Then, your self-talk pipes up.

What am I thinking? I don't have the skills. I'm not experienced enough. I'm too old/too young. What if I fail? How will I pay the mortgage/school fees/rent? How will I get clients? Who's going to listen to me? I don't know where to start. The banks won't lend me any money. What if someone gives me a bad rating? I don't know how to employ people. What if I start prioritising the business over my loved ones? How would I get the kids to school? The kids will think I don't love them anymore. This could break my marriage. What if I get sick?

You will probably be halfway through the above list, giving way too much air-time to your self-talk before realising it's your own Nasty Nan speaking. When you catch her, smile and say, "Thanks, Nasty Nan. No need to worry. I've got this. It's okay."

When you spot statements your self-talk is firing at you such as, "You don't have the experience to change," replace it with a new statement. Say, "I'm a smart woman who learns quickly and embraces change, and if I don't know the answer, I'll ask."

Stick that statement up everywhere—on your bathroom mirror, computer, etc.—so every time you catch your self-talk wittering on about how inexperienced you are, you have a counter-comment ready to fire back. Even if you don't believe it yet, say it. It's all about reprogramming your subconscious brain. Say it again and again. Alternatively, use the app Voice Loop to record a message to yourself outlining your new beliefs and reminding yourself what a beautiful, capable woman you are.

I know this sounds odd, and I refused to do it for months. My Nasty Nan was in full swing at that time. When I did eventually record a message for myself on Voice Loop, it was so lovely to hear and brought such a smile to my face. It can really help you reprogram your subconscious. So go on; give it a go.

If you have a supportive partner or friend, share this technique and the name of your self-talk with them. If in conversations you sound stressed, depressed, or defeated, get them to ask, "Who is talking? You? Or your self-talk?"

My partner does this with me. If I'm rabbiting on about all the reasons why I can't do my next business venture, he just smiles and says, "Nasty Nan is on fire today," which acts as a handy circuit breaker to stop myself spiralling downwards into a ravine of rubbish.

No one can make you feel inferior without your consent.
–Eleanor Roosevelt

Step 3: Filter

Now that we know the calibre of thoughts coming in, it's time to reduce their impact. Another technique is a straightforward filtering process. As a thought comes into your head, ask yourself the following:

Useful or not useful?

If it's not useful, physically and metaphorically breathe the thought away.

Conceptually, this is a simple exercise to understand, but like all techniques, it requires practise to make it a habit. You owe it to yourself to make this practice work for you. To remind yourself you are in armed combat with your self-talk, start wearing a ring, bracelet, or watch on your opposite hand. It will feel strange at first, which is the point. Every time you see your ring, bracelet, or watch, remind yourself you are filtering your self-talk into the useful thought, *I need to pick up the dry cleaning,* or the not useful, *I'm fat.* When you have these negative thoughts, simply take a deep breath in and smile. As you release, let go of them.

Knives are another fabulous reminder of combat with your self-talk. We see knives every day in our kitchen and out for dinner or lunch. Every time you see a knife, consider which end of the knife you should pick up. Go on; look at a knife. Let's think about this for a moment.

There are two ends—one sharp and pointy and one round and comfortable. You have a choice as to which end you hold. Select the sharp end, and you may well cause yourself injury. It will be really uncomfortable, and the knife won't be useful. Select the handle, and suddenly you have a powerful tool. It's such a difference, and it all comes down to choice. Start to do exactly the same with your self-talk. Listen to the useful stuff, and don't waste a second of the day on the nonsense your self-talk tells you.

Step 4: Fact or fiction?

Many of us allow our self-talk to fill in the blanks of our knowledge with stories—bad stories—on which we deliberate for weeks or even months.

A classic example is convincing yourself after going on a date, *He didn't call back the next day because he doesn't like me. Why would he like me when I'm (fill in the blank)?*

This is an example of a story not based on facts, but assumptions. Now, you could be right. You went on the date, and maybe yes, he's just not into you and doesn't have the manners, balls, or decency to send you a text. This can be confusing and hurtful. But here are some other possibilities: he could be shy, busy at work, giving you a bit of time, doesn't want to pressure you, or simply lost your number. Maybe his mate said he should wait five days so as not to seem too keen. Possibly, he hoped you might call him first, and when you didn't, he thought you didn't like him. Do you get where I'm coming from?

The *best* solution, if you accept you are a storyteller (which we all are, to some degree), is to get into the habit of finding out the facts quickly and avoid making assumptions. In this case, the easiest option is to call him (providing you want to catch up again), and ask if he would like another date. He can answer yes or no. Let me tell you, if he answers no, it will be *far* less painful than the miserable stories your self-talk will be telling you. Trust me on this!

Don't make shit up; it's that simple.

Step 5: Stop catastrophising

A bit like storytelling, this fictional self-talk takes the situation to the extreme, and then we ruminate over it. I know; I was a master of this. Thankfully, today I'm quicker at spotting my catastrophising and find it easier to laugh at the absurdity of my statements, spending less time drowning in them. Here is a very real statement of mine.

At age six, my son struggled greatly with reading at school. Yes, it was a real concern, and some action needed to be taken to help him. All of this is valid. However, my catastrophising self-talk went like this:

My son can't read in year two, which means he'll become an illiterate teenager and drop out of school, which will lead to him becoming addicted to drugs and result in suicide.

I went from not reading to death in seconds!

As I write this, I laugh...initially. It is, after all, such an absurd statement. Then I feel sad; this is classic catastrophising in action, and let me tell you, it was very real for me and extremely exhausting. I spent many a night picturing my happy six-year-old as a drugged-out teenager standing on a ledge somewhere about to jump, simply because reading wasn't his thing.

To overcome catastrophising, your sense of humour is *vital*. You really do need to laugh at yourself to see this self-talk has gone to extremes. I sometimes share my catastrophising thoughts with my teenagers. They are great levellers who say, "That's a bit crazy, Mum, even for you!"

If you don't currently have someone in your life to use as a sounding board, be your own. When catastrophising occurs, smile to yourself. You are being extreme. Then, ask yourself what a wise person would say. Think of someone who has always given you sage advice, and consider what their response might be. I used to have an aunt named Madge. She was my godmother, a very down-to-earth Yorkshire woman, who would call it straight. No fluff, no guff. So, if I were to ask myself, *What would Aunt Madge say?* I'd get a very wise response back (if not a little blunt).

Step 6: Reframing

Our self-talk can be very definitive as I am sure you have noticed. Our self-talk sees in black and white. Thoughts such as, *I'm overweight,* imply being overweight is part of who we are, and we will be overweight forever. If we were to add the words "at the moment" to the end of that sentence, it implies we are not *defined* by being overweight, and it could change at any moment.

Here's another example: *I can't swim.* This implies you'll never be able to swim. If you add the word "yet" on the end of the statement, it then becomes, *I can't swim* yet, and opens up your subconscious to all sorts of possibilities of learning to swim. The language we use with ourselves can be limiting and negative or open and positive. It's a choice, and it's important we use the right language with ourselves as well as others.

I found this a particularly great technique to pass on to teenagers. It is a technique they seem to be open to taking on board.

Step 7: Reaching out

If you realise your self-talk is spinning out of control, and you have tried to quiet the incessant chatter but it's still loud and clear, pick up the phone and call a friend or family member. If they are not available, call a support line or counsellor. Don't put up with the rubbish your self-talk throws at you. You are a wonderful woman worthy of so much more.

If you need help and no one is around, please flip to the back of the book for a table of support numbers in the index (page 98). They are there to listen. You are not alone.

These seven steps are designed to help you find peace and harmony in your head and to create space for your beautiful intuition to come through.

Persistence is vital in muzzling our Inner Bitches, and I know you have that capability within. Think about losing your car in a car park. I specialised in this for a period of time, mainly because when my son was younger, he was great at finding the car. He would find the car as my daughter and I chatted on the way back from shopping. This meant I stopped paying attention to where I parked. Realising you've lost your car is super irritating. You think, *Okay, let's try level three. Over on the right? Nope. Over on the left? Nope. Okay, let's try level four. Over on the right? Nope.*

You get the picture; it's a series of failures until you eventually find your car. It's annoying, frustrating, and time consuming. Believe me, I know. But the point is, you don't give up. You don't catch a cab home, and when your partner asks, "Where's the car?"

you say, "Oh, I couldn't find it, so I caught the bus." No, that doesn't happen; you persist until you find it. But when it comes to self-talk, we lack persistence as soon as our self-talk says, "You can't do that." We go, "Oh, okay," and stop immediately. If you can be persistent and find your car in a car park, even if it takes you hours and has you in tears, I'm telling you, you can silence your self-talk. When you do, you will be able to hear your intuition, and your intuition has your back.

Chapter 5: Oxygen Suckers, Get Out!

Life is too short for shallow friendships.
–Aristotle

We have spent our time together so far looking within, which is really important work. Your relationship with yourself is key to thriving, and like mastering any new technique, self-compassion is an ongoing and daily practice to be successful. Keep taming your self-talk, and keep delegating, simplifying, or dumping tasks that seem to magnetically be attracted to you, even when they shouldn't be. Time saved through DSD should be used wisely on *you*. And absolutely give yourself those special, daily self-hugs.

We are now going to move outwards and spend the next few chapters looking externally at our world. We will help you succeed by creating strong, healthy boundaries in all aspects of your life.

People

When we look at the people in our life—our family, friends, and those we work with—there will be two extremes of people, and the rest fit somewhere in the middle, regardless of whether they are family, friends, or work colleagues. One type of person is someone you just love catching up with. They make you smile, feel lighter, and more energised. You look forward to seeing them and always feel refreshed afterwards. Then there is the other extreme, the person who gives you a sinking feeling in your stomach before you even catch up with them, and by the time you have left their company, you feel exhausted. It's like they sucked the living daylights out of you, and I call them "oxygen suckers." Now, our goal in life is to surround ourselves with people who make us feel energised and minimise the amount of time we spend with oxygen suckers.

There are two ways we can do this. Firstly, we can encourage people to behave how we want when they are around us, which will make them easier company, less draining, and more energising. Or, for those we feel are never going to change no matter how much we guide or encourage, they are true oxygen suckers. We then need to minimise the amount of time we spend with them by putting some boundaries in place.

It's important to stress you can't ultimately change people or control them—nor should you—but you *can* influence how they behave around you, and here are some fabulous tips to have in your relationship toolkit to help do just that.

Tip One: Let others know what you want; don't assume they just "get it."

When I run communication workshops, I ask participants what they want out of their relationships. What works for them, and what drives them crazy? Participants are always crystal clear with what they want, and they know exactly what drives them crazy.

"Brilliant," I say. "Now, have you told your partner, friend, colleague, or sister what you need?" The answer is nearly always the same: they haven't had that conversation mainly because they assumed the other person already knew. We can reduce so much tension in our relationships if we let those around us know what we want. They aren't telepathic, so tell them!

Tip Two: Encourage the behaviour you want.

My children are now lovely adults and were pleasant teenagers. This was partly because I was blessed to have easy-going children, but I was also very clear about what I wanted in terms of the way everyone spoke to each other in the home. Everyone had to be respectful, parent to parent, parent to child, child to parent, and sibling to sibling. As I used to say, "You don't have to love everyone in this house, but you do need to communicate with respect."

This included how my daughter greeted us in the mornings. My daughter isn't a morning person. She would wake up grumpy, and that set the tone in the house for the rest of the day. That didn't make me feel great; it wasn't respectful, especially since I was making breakfast for her. My daughter was asked to be respectful in the morning, and all she had to do when she got up was simply smile at us and say, "Good morning." No other communication was required. If my daughter managed a smile and saying "Good morning," I often put a thank-you note in her lunchbox as a "reward." This is an example of the psychological concept of positive reinforcement. It encourages the behaviour you want.

If my daughter couldn't manage a smile and saying "Good morning," she got over the top hugs and kisses from me, which would drive her nuts. This is an example of negative reinforcement which discourages the grumpy behaviour. It quickly became clear to my daughter the small effort required to smile and say "Good morning" was far preferable to dealing with mushy hugs and kisses from her mother.

Parents are constantly teaching their children how to behave, and we actually do this with everyone who surrounds us, but because we aren't usually conscious about doing it, we can inadvertently encourage the wrong behaviour. For example, we often over-help because we care and don't want someone to fail, but failure is part of the journey, and we all need to experience it to grow.

Doing your child's homework is a great case in point. I get it why you might feel a need to; you don't want to see your loved one struggle. But this can potentially teach your children not to think or try. It might mask a learning problem or even make them feel helpless.

Looking at the psychology behind the concepts of positive reinforcement (words of praise and appreciation), and negative reinforcement (being told off, sent to your room), without a doubt, you will have greater success encouraging the behaviour of others through generous positive reinforcement than being heavy-handed with negative reinforcement. Give too much of the latter, and people switch off and stop listening to you.

In order to utilise the skill of positive reinforcement, you need to be vigilant, spot people behaving how you want—or at least close to it, then be appreciative and rewarding of that behaviour. I learnt this when I was studying psychology at university and had two toddlers. I'd come home from university via picking up the kids from childcare, and, as I was not an organised mother, there was always a mad dash to cook something for my ravenous children who always threatened a meltdown. Just before cooking, I'd set up a game for them to play and go back to the kitchen.

Now, here comes the magic. When they'd been playing nicely for a couple of minutes and the house was quiet, the temptation was to stay in the kitchen and race on with dinner, but no, this is when you need to positively reinforce them. I had a box of stickers in the kitchen, and every so often (not every day; I'll explain why shortly), I'd reward them by giving them a sticker, often on their forehead because it sent them into peals of laughter. Then, I'd let them know I loved how nicely they were playing.

The challenge for most of us is that we are so busy, we don't notice when people are doing what we want around us. We let that opportunity to praise and express appreciation pass, which means the only time we comment about their behaviour is when we don't like what they're doing. That unbalanced feedback can just sound like whingeing. For positive and negative reinforcement to work, you must be way more generous on the positive with lots of sincere praise and appreciation. Otherwise, you won't be heard at all. Besides, most of us are starved of appreciation. Think about it— when was the last time someone expressed gratitude and appreciation for what you do? When you learn to be generous, you'll stand out as a rare gem in the crowd.

As William James, the founder of modern psychology, said, "The deepest principle in human nature is the craving to be appreciated."

Now, let's get back to why you shouldn't give the same positive reward day in day out, like the thank-you notes in my daughter's lunchbox. Basically, if you gave notes every day, they would lose their magic. This is explained by the psychological term "partial reinforcement extinction effect," which means learning under partial reinforcements. For example, only occasionally giving a toddler a sticker is actually more robust and effective than rewarding them all the time.

Tip Three: Reward the attempt, not the result.

Another important concept to have in your toolkit is to understand the psychological term "shaping." Shaping is used a lot in dog training, and personally, I think there are real similarities between teaching dogs, children, and adults. Shaping is rewarding behaviour that isn't quite right, but there was at least an attempt. By rewarding the attempt rather than the result, you actually reach the end result quicker. This is an especially important concept to apply if you are a perfectionist.

For example, if you command a puppy to sit and it even just slightly lowers its bottom to the ground, you reward the puppy with a treat and gently push its bottom all the way down. This encourages the dog to quickly learn to sit. "Shaping" becomes even more important with more complex tasks when it's not as easy to get right the first time.

Let's look at getting a child to start loading the dishwasher. Now, I'm sure a perfectionist will have a "right" way to stack a dishwasher, but in reality, there are many ways, albeit some better than others. Imagine this scenario: a parent asks a child—let's call him Henry—to stack the dishwasher. The parent has "their way" of stacking; big plates to the left, little plates to the right, and so on. The parent might've explained where everything should go, but to someone who has never stacked the dishwasher before, they're probably just thinking, *Gee, there are a lot of plates* and, *I hope I don't drop any.* In other words, Henry has stopped listening to your instructions as he surveys the task at hand.

The good news is, Henry does as he is asked; he stacks the dishwasher, and from a psychological "shaping" point of view, this is a superb first step. The child is in action and should be rewarded with appreciation. "Thanks, Henry. Lovely to have your help. It makes me feel valued."

If the plates come out still a bit dirty because they weren't stacked properly or from not being scraped free from excess food, this is a learning moment for Henry. He now has the opportunity to learn by failing the first time; he can get it right the next time.

Here is the opportunity for some gentle guidance on what the dishwasher needs. Of course, sell Henry on the fact that if he does these extra small steps now, like scraping off excess food and stack with some space, the dishwasher will clean properly, and it will reduce rework for him later. This is the "ideal" way to start helping Henry with the dishwasher. But what often happens in practice is, Henry goes to stack the dishwasher then gets told off for not doing it the "right way." His being told off is negative reinforcement which dissuades Henry from doing the dishwasher again.

Adults can also come to blows over dishwashers. At the time, I was living with my boyfriend. Having filled the dishwasher after dinner, I went to get a couple of stray dishes from the table. On returning to the kitchen, I discovered my partner taking out *all* the plates and re-stacking my stacking. Negative reinforcement in action! I wasn't a five-year-old; my stacking was fine. I was surprised how cross I felt. My thought process was along the lines of, *Well, if you want the chore done, you can do it yourself,* which just goes to show how easy it is to discourage the behaviour you want, hence we need to be vigilant about what we encourage or discourage.

This takes me on to the next fabulous technique.

Tip Four: Explain the "why."

In many ways, this is an expansion of the first tip, but the key difference is the other person knows what you want but missed *why* it's important, probably because you assumed they magically knew. Since they don't get the "why," they either don't do it in the way you want or don't do it at all.

Imagine you've had a lovely seafood dinner. You know the seafood scraps will smell if left at room temperature for too long, and you know the local rubbish collection is early tomorrow morning, so your logic is to put the scraps in the kitchen bin and then take the kitchen bin contents out to your street bin. That way, you won't need to worry about odour in the kitchen the next day. Smart logic. You assume your partner is thinking the same, so you say, "Will you put the seafood scraps in the bin?" then head off to bed feeling very happy with the evening.

The next morning, after a hot summer's night, you wake up to a rotting seafood smell; the scraps are still in the kitchen bin! As you race around the house opening every window, your conversation with your partner goes a bit like this:

"Why didn't you put the seafood in the bin?"

"I did!"

"Not *that* bin! The *outside* bin!"

"Oh, you didn't say that."

You see, you assumed your partner understood your logic—your "why"—but they didn't.

The expression "to assume makes an *ass* of *u* and *me*" is so true. Don't assume. Instead, explain, and one of the great things to expand on is the "why."

We have looked at how to encourage people to behave how we would like when they're around us. Another great skill to explore is setting firm boundaries in regard to people, workload, family, money, and time with self. For an individual to function near their peak, they need to be able to afford themselves some downtime to recharge. This can't happen if you're expected to do everything for everyone or are surrounded by people who don't make you feel valued and supported.

For the rest of this chapter, we are going to talk about setting boundaries with the people in your life. Who do you let in? Who do you *need* to let into your life? Who do you *want* in your life? It's time to take stock of those around you. Are you surrounded by the right people for you, and have you "taught" them to behave correctly?

Having healthy relationships is key to a successful life. We can't—and shouldn't—expect to do everything on our own. We deserve people to be there for us, to support us in times of need.

We are worthy of having people who want us to be successful and celebrate our successes. We grow when people stimulate our thoughts and positively challenge our ideas, and we deserve fun people to hang around with. What we don't need and shouldn't put up with is people who drain our energy, don't have our best interests at heart, put us down, and resent our success. No, it's time these oxygen suckers are kicked out, and you might be surprised just how close to home they are.

There are oxygen takers and oxygen givers in life. Choose to surround yourself with those who help you flourish.

In her book *The Friendship Cure*, Kate Leaver cites some really interesting research. In a study published in the *American Journal of Public Health* in 2008, researchers found that women with strong social networks had a reduced risk of dementia.

As Leaver went on to point out, it's difficult to explain why this is the case, but the study is likely to suggest good friendships promote healthier behaviour.

Leaver's research also found we have a limited capacity for the number of friends we can manage, and I personally suspect this diminishes as we get older. In her research, she highlights some key numbers around relationships: one and a half, five, ten, and thirty-five. While most people equal one, our partner equals one and a half. Depending on how you look at it, they give a little more love or take up a little more time. Either way, they're worth a bit extra. Then comes our inner circle of five friends. Next is our close circle of ten friends. And finally, our outer circle of thirty-five friends. The rest are acquaintances.

It is these groups we are going to do a stocktake of. Who should we be investing time in to keep or bring into our inner circles, and who is sucking up too much of our valuable time with little to no reward returned? Some people in these groups will include family members. All groups will need to be examined so we can accurately ascertain who is sucking up your time unnecessarily, regardless of family or friend status. We will consider who we would like to invest more time in and who we would like to spend less time with.

Check in for a moment with your self-talk here; what is she saying? How do you feel about stocktaking your family and friends?

a. Excellent. I'm ready. Let's do it!

b. Oh, dear me. I don't want any confrontation by culling. It's easier just to put up with them.

If you answered "A," fabulous! Let's launch into it.

If you answered "B," stay calm. We aren't going to have any confrontations or big blow-outs with anyone. This is going to be a covert operation. No one will be the wiser as to what is going on. It's subtle, yet powerful. Relax, and enjoy the process.

Let's have a quick chat again about our conditioning as covered in chapter three.

Generations of women have been conditioned to be the dutiful daughter, wife, sister, aunt, niece, employee, etc. Although it's our choice who we help, don't help, and do or don't hang around with, our conditioning blinds us. We can end up surrounding ourselves with unhealthy people. It's time, as a grown woman, to do a stocktake on those surrounding you. If it turns out some members of your family or friends are unhealthy for you, it is time to send them love and metaphorically let them go. It doesn't have to, nor should it be, a vicious argument or nasty words. Instead, just like with your self-talk, you simply need to accept who is not right for you and release them to your "acquaintance" circle.

Mentally releasing these people out to your acquaintance circle is you validating to yourself that this person, for whatever reason, isn't right for you, and you are worth more. You have changed your perception and expectations of who they are; they aren't the wonderful friend or family member you'd hoped they would be. Letting them go stops disappointment and gives you permission to stop trying. It's exhausting trying to make a relationship work when it is so one-sided.

I know many women find this hard. They feel guilty letting go of people, especially family. We are conditioned to stick with family and are often assigned the role of peacekeeper, the organiser of events, the baker of cakes, etc. The internet is full of happy, lovey-dovey quotes about families.

Around Easter and Christmas, supermarket advertising is full of these happy family images of coming together to celebrate, and hey, if you are one of those women who has a lovely family like this—enjoy. Savour every minute of their company. For the rest of us, family can be a bit of a mixed bag; we can have a few suspect family members or a totally suspect family.

I used to know a woman in the UK—we'll call her Belinda— who had a suspect family. It was a big family. Having such a small family growing up, I used to look at Belinda's family with rose-tinted glasses. They looked just like the advertisements on television, all laughter and smiles. I often got invited to their family events—gosh, they were fun—and I'd see a band of happy people, all extremely photogenic.

They say the camera never lies, but let me tell you, it did on this occasion. The big smiles in those photos masked a very different story: bullying from childhood in subtle, toxic ways that continued into adulthood; parents' denial of their daughter's rape by a family friend; drug abuse and bankruptcy caused by one sibling to another. That family was a movie in and of itself, and it was really toxic for Belinda. I used to say to her, "You need to sack your family," and yet she kept going back for more social events and cooking for ungrateful parents. Each time, she came back feeling less self-worth.

It took Belinda years to break the bond her family had over her. She finally allowed herself to move her family into the "acquaintances" circle and mentally distance herself from them, which was much healthier for her. Now, she turns up briefly to a few family events a year simply to keep her children connected with their cousins. This has been a journey for Belinda, who now admits she should have let them go years ago, but that's easy to say, and I'm not saying this is easy. I simply want you to understand you have a choice in who you hang around with.

If the relationship isn't right for you, it's unlikely to be right for them, either. It can turn out, despite your best intentions, your care and support towards someone is actually enabling their bad behaviour to continue. They probably don't like how you make them feel, or what you seem to bring out in them. By letting them go, as well as doing yourself a huge amount of good, you will also be doing them a huge favour.

With anyone you move to your outer circle of acquaintances, you'll still be able to have polite, friendly conversations at big family gatherings, just like you would with other friends and family in your acquaintance circle. The difference is, there is no longer a need to invest your time and energy into maintaining them in your inner circle. Importantly, you have given yourself permission to disconnect emotionally. Your expectations are changed; you are no longer suffering disappointment after disappointment.

Family members and friends we let go aren't necessarily bad people. They are dealing with their own demons we can't control. This is why we send them love, forgive them in our heart, and then let them go. We can't control their journey in life, but we can control ours.

A woman I went to university with did just that with her mother. Jodie was a very attractive woman, but her mother saw her differently. She continually called her fat, amongst other things. Jodie and her father had a tight, loving relationship when he was alive, and I suspect Jodie's mum had always been jealous of that bond.

One Monday morning in the university canteen, we were chatting about our weekends. She told me of the torrid verbal abuse her mother doled out when she visited that weekend. I asked Jodie why she continued to visit, and as I sipped my coffee that day, little did I realise the profound effect that question would have on her.

Jodie kept wondering why she continuously visited her mother now that her father had passed away. Guilt? Duty? Whatever the reason, it prompted Jodie to slowly back away from visiting her mother. No discussions were had. Jodie felt it would serve no purpose, and I suspected she was right. She changed her expectations of her mother, moved her to an outer circle, and minimised one-on-one time.

Parents are real people. Some are healthy for us, and some aren't. Some can adapt to an adult relationship from a parent-child relationship, and some can't. That's okay. We have a choice as to how much time and effort, both physical and mentally, we choose to put into these relationships.

Now that we have the big family discussion out of the way, how do you tackle this calibration of your inner circle? Your goal here is to have the right people for you in your inner circles. Maintaining these circles requires effort, and this effort should be put into people worthy of it.

Exercise:

This exercise, like many, needs time and space to complete. You might want to revisit your thoughts over the coming week so you come from a place of intuition and not self-talk.

Consider all the people you know in circles:

Partner (1.5)→ Inner (5)→ Close (10)→ Outer (35)

Write a list of people you interact with on a regular basis, and allocate them to the group you believe they are in at the moment. This includes friends and family.

- Of these people, who sees you and loves you for who you are?
- Who helps you be the best version of yourself through support, encouragement, and honesty?
- Who loves your spirit?
- Who makes you feel energised when you see them?
- Who is there for you when the going gets tough?
- Who is delighted when you are successful?

Anybody can sympathise with the sufferings of a friend, but it requires a very fine nature to sympathise with a friend's success.
–Oscar Wilde

Whoever received a yes to questions five and six are absolute gold. If they aren't in your close circles already, it would be prudent to invest more time in cultivating these relationships. Be truly grateful for having these people in your life, and if you haven't done so recently, let them know how thankful you are for their company.

Right! We've got that list sorted, and now we come to the slightly more awkward part. Consider the family and friends who your intuition has always told you don't actually make you feel good. It's time to be honest with yourself. Listen to your heart.

- Who is draining?
- Who makes you feel tired after you have spent time with them?
- Who is too self-centred and makes everything all about them?
- Who envies your success rather than encourages it?
- Who always finds a way to jokingly put you down?
- Who overrides your conversations with their own opinions?
- Who seems too busy when help is required?
- Who doesn't appreciate what you do for them?

Take a couple of deep breaths, and tap into your intuition. Go through each of the questions above, one by one, and listen to the answers your intuition gives you. If in any of your responses you say, "I *should* stay in touch with...," "I *should* help...," "I *should* ring...," immediately discount it. That is your self-talk coming from a place of fear: fear of getting in trouble, of being alone, or being judged. Instead, listen to your intuition. It will come from your heart, and it will know immediately who is right for you and who isn't. When you tap into your intuition, this becomes an easier exercise than you first thought.

Your responses can promote different emotions. Just sit with these emotions. You might feel overcome with joy; finally, you are giving yourself a break from those painful afternoon teas or dreadful dinners. For others, it may bring up sadness to realise you have spent way too long hanging around people who aren't healthy for you. It is different for everyone. Sitting quietly, asking each of these questions individually, and giving your heart and intuition a chance to be heard, is one of the biggest gifts you can give yourself.

For some women, and I'd put myself in this category, there was a fear that, *If I sack too many friends, there will be no one left. I'll be on my own every Saturday night.* Be okay with this. Besides which, if we put FOMO (fear of missing out) aside, a night in with Netflix and takeaway has to be better than an expensive night out with someone who doesn't make you feel good. The wonderful aspect of this exercise is when you *do* free up space for new people to come into your life, they have an uncanny way of finding you. Be assured of that.

Your relationships should be about love, not habit. Lose your bad habits and find better ones.

When we look back at our friendship groups, we might find we have some inherited friends: friends of the family, old university or school friends, work friends, and friends made through your children or other school mums. These friends may have served a wonderful purpose at the time they came into your life, but this does not mean they will continue to do so. I know I am eternally grateful for all the women I hung out with when my children were young. The adult company in the parks and playgrounds during playdates kept me sane, but things have changed. We've all grown up, and naturally, many of those relationships have moved on. That's okay. We are not being nasty by letting these friendships go.

Again, I can't stress enough you *do not* need to have a conversation with these people. Simply let nature take its course. Stop calling or texting them, and see what happens.

I did this with a woman I knew many years ago. We were friends and would hang out on a Friday night, go to the movies, dissect the week over a bottle of wine; it was lovely. Then things changed. I changed. I started having children. First one, then two. My life was consumed with nappies and a lack of sleep. She was having an affair at the time with an older, married man. I didn't have a problem with my girlfriend having an affair; it's not my role to judge. Although, I did think she was heading for heartache, as I didn't see him leaving his wife. I shared this concern with her, which was probably the first nail in the coffin of our relationship.

The second was, my conversation was boring. As much as I didn't want to talk about children when I went out, the fact was my two children consumed a massive chunk of my life. I really had nothing else to talk about. Our lives had taken different paths, and when we caught up, it just wasn't fun anymore. I stopped calling, and do you know what? She didn't call back.

When she didn't call back, if I'm honest, I felt sad and aggrieved, although I now understand that was my self-talk saying, "Why doesn't she like me? I need everyone to like me." As the weeks went by, I actually felt relief. We had released each other to move in different directions. No harsh words were said. If we saw each other today, we would still hug and smile, and it wouldn't be awkward, just different.

I have also noticed, as I enter the next stage of life, you can be very alone in company. I've been a social butterfly for most of my life and have always loved a big group of friends, parties, and social gatherings. Being divorced with two grown and independent children has changed me.

Firstly, I don't have the energy to maintain a large circle of friends anymore, and the truth is, I don't want to. Secondly, I am less tolerant of boring, polite conversation, so I have concluded a small handful of great friends is all I need. Excitingly, I'm learning to really embrace and appreciate my own company. An accepting relationship with yourself is one no one can take away from you. Lose the norms of who you *should* be spending time with, and instead listen to your instincts. Spend time with the right people for you. Creating space is an opportunity for someone new and exciting to come into your life.

And consider this—every friend was a stranger at first.

Chapter 6: Money In, Problems Halved

How has it gone, decluttering your family and friend groups?

For some, you may have decided to tweak your inner circles with just a few changes by easing back on the investment of time in one or two relationships. For others, this may be a confrontational stage of self-compassion leading to the understanding you have invited people into your life who aren't necessarily appropriate for you. This is a powerful realisation. It is also a painful one. Be kind, and don't beat yourself up. The first step is to create some distance between the people you feel may be toxic or draining in your life. Then, you can start to see what comes about with that space. It will be interesting to see if they change as a result of you stepping back.

Boundary-setting with your inner circles is beautiful self-compassion, and if you have found they now appear rather sparse, it means you have created space for some delightful new people. Enjoy this time with yourself. It's precious, and you will find others will quickly be attracted to you.

Now that you have started to work out who is "out" and who is "in," it's important to establish some boundaries within these relationships. We are going to look at two aspects in particular—money and responsibility—but you can see the theory can be adapted to all facets of these relationships.

Money in…

We make money a taboo topic we rarely discuss. In the article "Why Is Talking About Money More Taboo Than Sex?" Michelle Schroeder-Gardner presents some fascinating facts (2018).

A survey conducted by Ally Bank reveals 70 percent of Americans think it's rude to talk about money (Puchalsky 2015). In this reference, "money" encompasses the fact that people don't like to talk about how much they pay in rent, monthly mortgage payment, or even how much they spend on internet services. Schroeder-Gardner asks, "Why does your internet bill have to be secretive?"

Schroeder-Gardner goes on to cite a survey done by Fidelity that shows 43 percent of respondents don't know how much their partner earns, and 36 percent are unaware of the amount they have invested—which is scary ("2015 Couples Retirement Study Fact Sheet" 2015). I'll talk about that in a moment.

Schroeder-Gardner's research then gets even more bizarre, as a study by a University College in London found people were *seven* times more likely to talk to a stranger about sex, affairs, and sexually transmitted diseases than discussing their salary! Totally weird!

Clearly, there is a taboo around money, and it's probably due to the conditioning from our Victorian forbearers. As the historical author V. L. McBeath points out, for women today, it's hard to picture the lack of rights women had to endure in the Victorian era, especially their lack of rights involving money. It was only 150 years ago, in the midst of the Victorian era, where women were conditioned to see themselves only as homemakers, nurturers, and caregivers. They were viewed by society as emotional, unstable, and incapable of making rational decisions, and this was shockingly backed up in the eyes of the law. Once a woman got married, all her possessions were given over into her husband's control (2020). You can see, for women like our great-grandmothers and even our grandmothers, money wasn't high on their agenda because it wasn't allowed to be. All that conditioning and learned helplessness surrounding money have been passed down through generations. We've inherited much of it, like my grandmother's belief that it's "unladylike to talk about money." It's important we're the circuit breakers of this conditioning, not only for our own financial well-being but to ensure our sons and daughters also have a healthy relationship with money.

Let's take a step back to chapter three and our childhood conditioning. I was heavily conditioned about money by my grandmother. Looking back on her life, it had been tough financially; she'd lived through two world wars, the Great Depression, and her husband's failed business. Not surprisingly, she always came from a lack of money.

Her frugality was insane. From a sustainability point of view, it was magic. From a conditioning point of view, not so beneficial. I regularly heard, "Money is the root of all evil," "Money doesn't make you happy," "Money doesn't grow on trees," and, "It's unladylike to talk about money." It's that last comment I now reflect on the most. My grandmother was a smart woman, and I wonder where we would have been if she had taken the financial reins. Don't get me wrong—my grandfather was a good man, but he wasn't a businessman. If I think about the sharpness my grandmother had before dementia set in, she would have been a perfect businesswoman. Nothing would have gotten past her; she would have made every penny work. But my grandmother's conditioning was such that she left all the financial stuff to her husband and baked, knitted, and played cards. The results speak for themselves.

I know you'll be saying, "But it's changed, Tracey. We are in a different era."

Yes, you're right. Things have changed. Women have equal rights and more opportunities in the workplace than ever before, and I'm absolutely delighted the pay gap in Australia between men and women is closing. This is fabulous news. There is still a gap, but we are trending in the right direction.

The questions I raise are: Have we, as women, changed our attitude and responsibility involving money? Are we different from my grandmother, or are we still deferring to our partners? Is there financial parity in our homes?

You see, we never know what goes on behind closed doors. We assume everyone has the same relationships and arrangements as us. We might be closing the divide on the pay gap, but I don't believe that necessarily reflects in the home. Until we reach parity in the home, it's not going to make any real difference to women.

When I was married, I am embarrassed to say, I was just like my grandmother. I happily left the financial stuff to my husband. I really dislike Excel. I'm not a detail-oriented person. I put my head in the sand and absolved myself of responsibility, which wasn't a great strategy. I was just lucky to have married an honest man.

Leaving the finances to your partner does not absolve you of the responsibility of those finances. This is one task you need to step up to and handle either yourself or jointly, otherwise it may have catastrophic consequences for you.

I know a woman who is very smart—university qualified, who found this out the hard way. The first time she realised her husband had a serious gambling problem was when the bailiffs came to take her house and all of its contents!

Just think about that for a moment. You just got the kids to school, you're wiping down the kitchen bench, and there's a knock at the door. You answer the door, and your life changes forever. You're instantly homeless. You have nothing more than a couple of bags of clothes. And if you don't think it could happen to you, she didn't think it would happen to her, either.

As a woman, it is *not* appropriate to be kept in the dark financially, and ignorance is not a defence.

The point is, you owe it to yourself to be financially compassionate to yourself, and part of that is being knowledgeable about your financial situation.

I raise this point because the more I explore this area, the more I find there isn't financial parity in the home. We, as women, can be part of the problem.

Another sorry tale I came across a couple of years ago was from another beautiful woman, Sandra. Sandra volunteered at a local hospice in the UK, and I have always been in awe of the compassionate work she did with the terminally ill. She, like me, didn't enjoy the paperwork of marriage, and I recollect one time laughing about how much we hated Excel as a software tool. I shudder now at that very conversation. If she had been proactive in keeping an eye on her joint finances, she would have noticed substantial amounts of money being syphoned out of their investments. This went on for a couple of years, and then her husband left for another woman, and he left her with debt.

I know these seem like extreme examples, but the point I want to stress is not about partners doing wrong; we can't control what others do, but we *can* control the impact others have on us if we take responsibility for our finances. Taking control of your finances reduces any financial worry. You will sleep better when you take your head out of the sand.

The same is true if you are in business with a partner or friend. I recall going to a business course over twenty years ago. It was a weekend course, so it wasn't too detailed, which I naturally appreciated. Despite the course being so long ago, one point the facilitator made stood out: if you go into business with a partner or friend, dot the i's and cross the t's as if you are going into business with an archenemy. This advice sounded a little harsh at the time, but it has stuck with me, and I now truly understand his sage words.

An old client of mine, Francis, was in business with her husband in the UK. She was the brains of this logistics business, and, if you like, he was the brawn. He was a great networker; he could open doors—a vital part of growing a business. Given her logistics smarts, do you think she was smart with finances? Sadly, as it turns out, no. Love made her blind. I only became aware of this after numerous coaching sessions; we were talking about the challenges of cash flow in business. During this conversation, something triggered Francis, and the floodgates opened and tears poured out. It turns out, her husband had made several investments over the years without her knowing, one by fraudulently signing her name. He had nearly sent her bankrupt twice! And now, she had gone into business with him and was fearful he would embezzle money from their company. I know. I hear you; it's hard to fathom why she would go into business with him in the first place when she knew what he was like. As I say, she loved him, and he did bring complimentary skills to the business, despite the massive trust issues surrounding money. I counselled Francis to get legal advice, to understand her rights in the business and her marriage, and to ensure every "i" was dotted and every "t" was crossed to protect her assets. Francis's business is still going, but has the issue been resolved? Who knows? Shortly after that conversation, she stopped coming to see me. Too close for comfort, maybe?

When children come along, a common situation many women can find themselves in, as some are the primary caregiver for their children (which, as far as I'm concerned, is the hardest job of all), they may only have either part-time work or none at all. This typically means their full-time partner earns more than them, which is okay. Raising a family takes teamwork. Unfortunately, as my financial advisor pointed out, behind closed doors, archaic attitudes are still held in many homes:

- "I earn more money than you. What I do with it is my affair."
- "I earn more money than you, so I can spend more money on me."
- "You don't need to worry your pretty little head with money stuff. You have a nice house, don't you?"
- "You don't need to know what I earn."
- "You don't need to read the document; I just need you to sign it!"

Yes, it's the twenty-first century, and I have been astounded to hear these statements are still being made.

I want to be very clear. These attitudes are not acceptable, are not supported by the law, and it may indicate something more sinister at play: financial abuse.

According to White Ribbon Australia, below are some examples of financial abuse:

- Someone taking complete control of finances and money
- Restricting access to bank accounts
- Providing an inadequate allowance and monitoring what their partner spends money on
- Forbidding a partner to work
- Taking a partner's pay and not allowing them to access it
- Preventing them from getting to work by taking their keys or car
- Identity theft to secure credit
- Using their credit card without their permission
- Refusing to work or contribute to household expenses

If you feel some of these situations may apply to you, go to the index (page 155), and contact one of the numbers to get the support you deserve.

It's a bit like domestic abuse. We don't know what's happening to our friends and family behind closed doors because people don't like to talk about money.

If you aren't clear about finances in your relationship, let me walk you through the basis of the law here in Australia. If you live in another country, be proactive and find out your rights.

Unlike when my grandmother was alive, the law is now more equitable. If you are in a "de facto" relationship for more than two years, or if you are married, your assets become your partner's assets and vice versa. Referred to as a "common pool," all debts become part of that pool with your partner. If you don't have transparency to this pool, including how much is coming in and going out, you won't know what is fair and right for you to have, especially if there is a time when it needs to be divided.

You have a right to know how much your partner is earning and what investments or debts you both or individually have. Your partner has the same rights. If you don't know, ask. If they don't want to tell you or fob you off, your inner alarm bells should be ringing. You *have* to step up; it's important.

I know this isn't easy, and our conditioning doesn't help. I really want you to understand it's never too late to start. When you're clear about what is going on and in the driver's seat of your finances, it will *always* put you in a better position financially.

If you don't know where to begin, I would highly recommend *The Barefoot Investor* by Scott Pape. It's a fabulous starting point.

Now that the heavy conversation with money is done, it's time to consider your relationships between money, friends, and family. Consider those in your inner circles, and ask yourself if the split of "giving" and money is appropriate.

I moved one friend to an acquaintance circle because of his tightness with money. He never offered to buy a round. We always split the bill, or he would let me pay. I found his tightness unattractive. Everyone joked about it, often to his face, which he never seemed to take offence to. He was almost proud of it, and I get why. Mugs like me spent years paying for his drinks and dinner because we couldn't bear the pain of going through the bill item by item. So, who was the fool?

A girlfriend of mine also fell prey to over-generosity. She was a single mum who had always lived close to the poverty line, yet you'd invite her over for dinner, and she'd bring a glorious cheese platter. Now, don't get me wrong, the cheese platters were always lovely, but it had to have set her back over one hundred dollars, at least. The last thing I wanted was for her to spend that amount of money on a cheese platter. It went against the purpose of the invitation, which was for her to enjoy a free meal. It's taken a while, but we have finally struck a deal. An inexpensive bottle of wine is perfect for her to bring along and nothing else.

We can look at generosity as an action that comes from a generous place. In other words, if you have a full bank account, freezer, and can afford to share, this is what you can do. This is very different from the concept of over-giving: giving when we are short of what we are giving, be it time, money, or stuff. We over-give because we need to feel good about ourselves, to be appreciated or loved, or to be seen as the better person. We hope for a return on what we give. It stops us from feeling guilty or thinking we should (Jacobson 2018).

There are several flaws with these arguments, the main ones being:

- Over-giving doesn't make us more likeable. In fact, it makes us more likely to be taken for granted.

- Over-givers are very attractive to the manipulative and aggressive or those who are needy and refuse to take responsibility.
- Over-givers typically find it hard to receive, so even when reciprocated, it's likely to be rebuffed. I did this with my "tight" friend on the one rare occasion he actually offered to pay for a meal. I bizarrely turned him down. "No, don't be silly," I'd said. What was I thinking?
- Over-givers damage their self-esteem by trampling over their own boundaries.

The thing is, we get into social habits. Some of us are quicker to put our hand in our pockets for drinks, taxis, coffees, etc., and others aren't. Just take stock of your general money habits for a moment, then consider your inner circles.

- Who do you need to pull back from financially and let them pay?
- Who do you need to step it up with?
- How generous are you to yourself with money? Are you overspending to make yourself feel better, or are you miserly when it comes to yourself?
- What are your new boundaries?

Now, if you have children, this bit is for you.

The love we have for our children can blind us in terms of making sound financial decisions towards them. When they are little, it's obvious you pay for everything, but as they get older, they need to be able to contribute and manage their own funds.

I grew up with love but not much money, and from a very young age, I always knew my mum was stressed financially. As a result, I never asked for much, and as soon as I could work, I did. My first paying job was at sixteen, working at the local sports centre. I saved and saved my pay and eventually had enough to buy a record player with a built-in radio and cassette player. I felt very cool owning it. There was tremendous satisfaction in buying that record-player. I mean, I'm still talking about it now. I understood the importance of saving and working to get the things I wanted in life. It was a wonderful lesson overly generous parents rob their children of.

As a mother, I know there is part of me that doesn't want my children to be caught up with the stress of financial hardship like I grew up with, and because I love them, part of me wants to give them everything. Another part of me wants them to value the importance of saving money, being frugal, and learning delayed gratification, which will set them up well in life. It's a fine line that continually shifts as they grow. What was appropriate last year will have changed this year. What I *am* clear about is, if I am overly generous, not only will they miss out on being financially empowered, I will teach them to take me and my wallet for granted, and that is not a good thing.

Consider the following questions below. There are no right or wrong answers. Your intuition will tell you where your boundaries should be.

- How much are you paying for your children's upkeep?
- Are they old enough to get a job?
- If they are driving your car, do they fill it up with petrol?
- Are they ordering Uber Eats on your card when there is a fridge full of food?
- If they aren't working but are over the age of ten (yes, ten; remember, you are their mother, not servant) are they contributing to running the house in non-financial ways such as cooking, cleaning, and maintenance?

Even a child who is now an adult can disrespect boundaries. I knew of a woman whose husband left her for another woman, but that's not the sad part. Her son in his early twenties considers the house he and his mother live in and her bank account to be his early inheritance! He bitches and complains about every cent she spends, including the grocery shop; he is a bully. Now, let's be clear again about the law. When your child is eighteen, you can ask them to leave. Legally, you don't need to support them, and you don't have to leave them anything in your will.

Have boundaries with those close to you. Otherwise, you will become the money tree my grandmother said didn't exist.

…Problems Halved

Really, it's a simple concept. Whose problem is it? Mine, yours, or ours?

This is a concept I have used numerous times in my coaching, and it's fascinating how blurred those lines can get, particularly for women who spend too much time dealing with problems, drama, and issues that aren't theirs to solve.

Everyone went to my mother with their problems. She was a beautiful soul who always had time for everyone except herself. She looked after elderly neighbours, helped friends with their foster children, looked after her elderly parents, looked after me, helped kids from dysfunctional homes who went to her school, and so the list went on. Now, I am not saying you should be an uncaring individual. Not at all. What I am saying is to know your boundaries and question whether your help is helping in the long run.

Tap into your intuition, not your self-talk, which loves being a martyr. Things to consider:

- Are you over-caring?
- Are you taking on things you shouldn't?
- Are you doing it for the wrong reasons? Out of fear, obligation, or to look good in the eyes of your mother-in-law?
- Is your well-intentioned help actually making them helpless?
- Are you aiding them to avoid responsibility?

- How much of your help is making them lazy?
- How much of your help is masking the real issue?

Let me explain further.

As previously mentioned, my gorgeous son struggled at primary school with reading, which affected all his other subjects. It was a lonely struggle for us, trying to find out what was going on for him and how we could close the gap. For many years, it was very much "our" problem, as I felt he needed my support and guidance to get the help he needed. When he went to high school, things changed. He had always been very obliging in going from one specialist to another, but like most children, he was less obliging in doing the exercises required. There were often tense conversations at home—nagging conversations, really—and I didn't like who I was becoming over the dinner table.

When he was in high school, I realised I couldn't keep pushing him along; he needed to own his academic results. I said to my son, "I already have two degrees. I don't need any more qualifications." School and his results were his journey, and he needed to step up. I let him know I'd always be there for him if he needed assistance; he just needed to ask, but his school work and progress were all up to him.

Two things happened.

First, it was a *massive* weight off my shoulders. I felt such relief I had stopped trying to control and drive something that was impossible for me to control. Phew!

Second, his grades tanked. I had been unwittingly masking the problem of his lack of effort. It became abundantly clear the current problem was he totally lacked motivation. It was a wonderful wake-up call for us both. He gradually stepped up, I was less stressed, and our relationship was so much better.

I see this regularly with women in the workplace. They genuinely care about their company, and when they see areas that aren't working, even if it's not in their jurisdiction, they go about fixing things. They stretch themselves so thin over so many areas, their own work starts to suffer. Instead of being patted on the back for trying to hold things together for the company, they end up having conversations with management about their own performance. The offenders are not discovered, as their poor performance has been unwittingly masked by a caring woman. All parties lose.

Sometimes, the kindest thing you can do is allow someone to fail. Failing is learning, and if you stop people from failing, you limit their growth and mask the true issue. My kids at primary school learnt "F.A.I.L." stands for "First Attempt in Learning," which I think is brilliant. What a pity this isn't lauded further on in life!

Know when you should take on a problem and when you should not. It's one thing to be a supportive listener and give appropriate guidance, it's another to take on someone else's problem as your own.

When I coach women on this subject, I recommend they have three items close by to remind them whose problem it is: mine, yours, or ours. You might wear three bracelets, have three smooth stones on your desk, three thin rings on a finger, or three flowers in a vase. Whatever you choose, it is worth investing in a visible reminder so you don't take on a problem that, quite frankly, isn't yours.

When a problem arises, pause for a minute and consider if the problem is theirs, yours, or a joint issue. We women tend to take problems on as our own because we can, we care, or think we'll do a better job. None of these are reasons for you to dive in and solve the issue.

Of course, men can fall prey to this, too. I coached a man named David several years ago. He was a director in a very successful finance company. The staff loved him; he had no airs or graces and was always approachable. In fact, he was too approachable. Everyone would go to him with their problems. Small or large, they went to David, and David always gave them a solution. I was brought in to coach him, as he had just had his *second* heart attack, and his specialist felt if he didn't change his ways, he might not be so lucky the next time.

To resolve people coming in with their problems, we stuck the phrase "Ask for a possible solution first" in bright yellow paper at the bottom of his computer screen, something *he* could see but employees couldn't. The aim was, every time someone came into his office with a problem, David would ask them to think about a possible solution themselves first, then come back if they still needed advice. David took a while but gradually adopted this behaviour. It was interesting what he noticed.

First, there was a dramatic drop in the number of people coming to see him. Second, he realised by always giving his employees the answer, he had inadvertently been teaching them not to think for themselves and dampening their confidence in their own ability. Finally, some solutions from the staff were ingenious. Yes, this did surprise him. Who'd have thought?

The other point here is, in addition to not physically taking on problems that aren't yours to take, don't mentally take them on either. That can be just as exhausting, if not more so. Going back to my son and his school performance, I could hand over the baton of school work responsibility to him, but if I still worry about how he is doing in my head, I am still holding on to that problem. This is actually worse because now I am worrying about something I have rightly given away control of, and that's stressful and crazy. Catch yourself if you find yourself mentally clinging onto problems that aren't yours. Send yourself some love, and let those problems go.

This chapter has been about being mindful of your money and choosing which problems you are going to take on. This mindfulness will increase the money you have in your purse and the time you have for yourself, which is perfect self-compassion.

Chapter 7: Become the Woman You Were Always Meant to Be

"If I want to be free, I've got to be me."
–Bob Proctor

Let's take stock of what you have achieved so far.

- You have delegated, simplified, and dumped your tasks (DSD).
- You've released yourself from unhelpful conditioning.
- You've wrangled in your self-talk, which means you can listen to your intuition.
- You're investing time with the right people.
- You're being smarter with your finances.
- You now know which problems you own and which you don't.

You have done so much cerebral sorting; it's incredible. Your life is taking shape nicely. There still might be some adjustments required, but stop for a moment and look at what you have achieved. Now you are ready to symbolically release the old you and invite the new brilliant you to come out and shine. To do this, you need to ensure you have a matching bright and sparkling self-image.

What do I mean by self-image? The discovery of self-image was first made in the 1960s by a plastic surgeon named Dr. Maxwell Maltz, who wrote the book *Psycho-Cybernetics* (1960). The book's title comes from "cybernetics," loosely translated from Greek (a helmsman who steers his ship to port), and "psycho," meaning "of the mind." So, the mind steers us towards a goal.

Maltz was performing plastic surgery on people well before nip and tucks, lifts, and implants became common vernacular. He operated on people with terrible facial disfigurements, distortion, or scarring. Maxwell noticed once the disfigurement was corrected, usually after three or so weeks, the patient demonstrated a dramatic change in character and a rise in self-esteem and self-confidence, which seemed to make sense. Maxwell also noticed not every patient demonstrated this psychological lift, even if the surgery was highly successful and the disfigurement was removed. Some patients remained no different at all psychologically, and some even felt worse. There was something else going on.

Further research led Maxwell to discover our self-image. No matter what we do on the outside, say correcting a facial disfigurement, there will be no dramatic psychological change unless there is a corresponding change to our self-image.

Our self-image is how we see ourselves. Our self-image defines our actions, feelings, and behaviour in life. It's our self-image the world sees, and ultimately, it's our self-image that dictates how successful we are. No matter how great your hair is, how expensive your outfits are, how much weight you lose, or if you go for a lift, tuck, or boob job, if you don't see yourself as successful, beautiful, and worthy on the inside, no one else will. Our self-image has total control over our ability to achieve or fail in life. The goal of this book has been to declutter and reshape you from the inside out to finally see yourself as the brilliant woman you were always meant to be. Changing our self-image is the final stage.

When I was introduced to the concept of self-image, it explained so much about a woman I used to work with. Vanessa was a slender, attractive woman with clear olive skin that always glowed. In addition, Vanessa was great company, easy to laugh with, smart (helped me greatly with Excel), and yet was always single. This started to become an issue for Vanessa as she headed into her mid-thirties and the window to have children was closing fast. She tried everything to find a partner (online dating hadn't really started): she went to social single meets, got her friends to organise blind dates, took up hobbies, and chatted to men in supermarkets. You name it, she tried it. But the same pattern emerged. Getting a date wasn't a problem, and finding great guys didn't seem to be a problem either; there was no end to the line of suitors, but turning the date into a long-term relationship was. Vanessa ended one seemingly well-matched relationship after another, much to our bewilderment. When I left that company, we went our separate ways, and I have often wondered how Vanessa did and if she had the family she dreamt of. Looking back now, I feel it could have been her self-image keeping her single. Her self-image (her internal thermostat) didn't want to be in a relationship for whatever reason. Maybe it was a fear of being hurt or not feeling worthy of love, but irrespective of the reason, the self-image sabotaged the relationship time and time again to ensure Vanessa got back to the "set-point" it was comfortable with: being slender and single.

If we want the rest of the world to see us as the wonderful women we are, we need to see ourselves as wonderful women. This concept of self-image finally explains to me the expression "beauty is in the eye of the beholder." If you see yourself as beautiful, the rest of the world will too.

Our self-image is about seeing ourselves as being perfectly imperfect and loving who we are today, right now as you are reading this book. If you aren't getting the results you want in life, it is likely your self-image needs an upgrade.

Unsurprisingly, our self-image has been subconsciously created from childhood conditioning, along with our past successes, and of course, what we recall most—our past failures.

All the work you have done to date—identifying blockers, limiting beliefs, examining childhood conditioning, and analysing and decluttering your self-talk—should give you fabulous insight into what your current self-image is. It's time she had a face-lift.

Step 1: Define your current self-image.

Our self-image reflects our results in life. Analyse your current results, and you will get a clear picture of what your current self-image is set at.

What are you like, generally?

Health: Are you mostly sick or healthy? Do you look after yourself? Are diet, alcohol, and/or sleep affecting your health?

Physical: Are you strong, weak, overweight, or underweight? Do you exercise?

Mental: Do you worry? Are you anxious, guilty, depressed, or happy-go-lucky?

Work: Has your career always been successful? Do you get paid well? Are you a workaholic?

Money: Does it run out as soon as it appears, or are you a master of amassing wealth?

Relationships: Are they typically good, bad, or indifferent? Are they supportive, caring, loving, and fun, or more on the oxygen sucking scale?

What have you gleaned from answering these questions? Where is your self-image currently set at? Just like a thermostat heats or cools the room to keep you at a particular temperature, your self-image is the same. Whenever you deviate from that set-point, your self-image works really hard to bring you back to that point.

If you have ever dieted, you know exactly what this is like. You find a new diet; you have tried them all: Atkins, Paleo, No-Carb, 5/2, and so many more. All show some weight loss at the beginning. It starts out exciting, but somehow, and you don't know how, that weight comes right back. The same is true of money. You save and save; the holiday fund is looking healthy—then *boom!* The car needs fixing, and you are back where you started.

Trust me; this is your self-image at play. In this case, your current self-image is set at you being overweight and broke, not worthy of wealth or losing weight, and no matter what you do, this is exactly where you will come back to. It's time for your self-image to change.

Capture your current perceived self-image by analysing your results to date in all areas of your life. Include in your analysis your past conditioning, all those limiting beliefs, and mean self-talk you have unwittingly been listening to for years.

Write out your current self-image; paint yourself a clear picture of her. As you do, it will become clearer what you want to release and what you want to keep. There will be lovely aspects you will want to keep. I, for instance, have always loved my compassion and my ability to assist others to be successful. I included that in my new self-image. My lack of worthiness around money was top on the list for me to release from my old self-image. Yes, Grandma, I'm talking about money again.

Capture a complete picture of your old self-image and how it reflects the results you are currently getting. Hold on to your old self-image paper for the moment.

Step 2: Create a new, improved self-image. What do you value?

To inspire your thoughts on how you would like to see yourself, your new self-image, we are going to explore what you value in life. Our values are like a moral compass, and they guide us in how we should live our lives. They give us direction and help us thrive, no matter what life throws at us. When we are not living by our values, it causes us stress, frustration, and anxiety.

- Pick values that resonate with you. Don't overthink; don't put what you think you *should* put down. Just go with your intuition. Add other values if they aren't on the list.

- You might find your values can be grouped. If they can, do so.

From each group, write the one value that stands out to you most. These are your top values.

As a guide, this is how I came up with my values. From the earlier list, these are the words that stood out for me in no particular order:

Challenge, Amusement, Acceptance, Appreciation, Bravery, Candour, Ethical, Fairness, Fortitude, Freedom, Fun, Gratitude, Liberty, Success, Equality, Daring, Spontaneity, Intuition, Compassion, Honesty, and Money.

I've grouped them like this:

Adventure, Challenge, Bravery, Fortitude, Daring

Fun, Spontaneity, Amusement

Compassion, Acceptance, Equality, Fairness, Ethical

Gratitude, Appreciation

Honesty, Candour

Freedom, Liberty

Success

Intuition

Money

The ones highlighted in bold are those that speak to me the loudest and are included in defining the new me.

Acceptance	Collaboration	Drive
Accomplishment	Comfort	Effectiveness
Accountability	Commitment	Efficiency
Accuracy	Common sense	Empathy
Achievement	Communication	Empowerment
Adaptability	Community	Energy
Adventure	Compassion	Enjoyment
Altruism	Competence	Enthusiasm
Ambition	Concentration	Equality
Amusement	Confidence	Ethicalness
Assertiveness	Connection	Excellence
Attentiveness	Consistency	Experience
Acceptance	Contentment	Exploration
Accomplishment	Contribution	Expressiveness
Accountability	Control	Fairness

Appreciation

Balance

Beauty

Boldness

Bravery

Brilliance

Calmness

Candour

Capableness

Carefulness

Certainty

Challenge

Charity

Cheerfulness

Cleanliness

Cleverness

Gracefulness

Gratitude

Greatness

Growth

Happiness

Hard work

Harmony

Health

Honesty

Honour

Conviction

Cooperation

Courage

Courtesy

Creativity

Credibility

Curiosity

Daringness

Decisiveness

Dedication

Dependability

Devotion

Dignity

Discipline

Discovery

Logic

Love

Loyalty

Mastery

Maturity

Meaning

Motivation

Openness

Optimism

Order

Organisation

Family

Fame

Fearlessness

Feelings

Ferociousness

Fidelity

Focus

Foresight

Fortitude

Freedom

Friendship

Fun

Generosity

Genius

Giving

Goodness

Responsibility

Restraint

Satisfaction

Security

Self-reliance

Selflessness

Sensitivity

Serenity

Service

Hope

Humility

Imagination

Improvement

Independence

Individuality

Innovation

Inquisitiveness

Insightfulness

Inspiration

Integrity

Intelligence

Intuitiveness

Irreverence

Joy

Justice

Kindness

Knowledge

Lawfulness

Learning

Liberty

Talent

Teamwork

Thoroughness

Thoughtfulness

Trustworthiness

Originality

Passion

Patience

Peace

Persistence

Playfulness

Power

Productivity

Professionalism

Prosperity

Purpose

Quality

Reason

Recognition

Recreation

Reflectiveness

Respect

Realism

Results

Reverence

Rigor

Risk-taking

Sharing

Simplicity

Sincerity

Skilfulness

Smartness

Solitude

Spirituality

Spontaneity

Stability

Status

Stewardship

Strength

Structure

Success

Support

Surprise

Sustainability

Timeliness

Tolerance

Toughness

Traditional

Tranquility

Transparency

Trust

Truthfulness

Understanding

Uniqueness

Unity

Vitality

Wealth

Winning

Wisdom

Step 3: Create the new you. Write your character description.

Now that you have identified your new values, incorporate them with elements from your old self-image, elements you hold dear, and then add new beliefs you have developed from previous chapters to reflect the woman you have always wanted to be. With all of this insight, write down your new self-image and the life she is now living. To make this easier for you, imagine you are writing a character description for the leading lady in a new movie. You are the leading lady, and this is your life movie. Write with detail to make it spring from the page and excite you. This new self-image should make you smile and your heart flutter; this is the woman you have been waiting to connect with for quite some time. You are going to write this new self-image in the present tense as if you are already her. Start your character description with the words, "I am so happy and grateful to have become the woman I was always meant to be. I am…"

Be positive and really descriptive of this brilliant woman, your new self-image, who is perfectly imperfect. You love her imperfections, just like a precious diamond, whose imperfections make it stand out from the crowd, creating greater depth and interest within. You, too, are wonderful just as you are. Don't worry about grammar or spelling, but do be as evocative as you can. You need to be able to picture her and her life. The more detail, the better. Write as if you are where you want to be, such as,

"I love being fifty-four kilograms," as opposed to, "I am going to lose weight."

Describe your health, your fitness, your weight, your looks, your mindset, your relationships, how you tackle life's curve balls, and how you approach new ventures. Describe the new you in detail so you are crystal clear on the woman you were always meant to be.

It is time you rose from the ashes ready to shine in the world once more.

Step 4: Release the old and embed the new.

When you have written out your old and new self-image, burn the old one. Literally and symbolically destroy it. Send her love, and send her on her way; she is no more. Stick the new self-image up somewhere, and read it out loud every morning and night.

Place reminders wherever you can to remind yourself of the wonderful woman you really are. It is important for you to start to believe you are her. You need to start behaving as her *now*! Today!

The expression "fake it until you make it" is perfect here. We are tricking your subconscious into believing this is the new you. We are changing the set-point of your self-image. If your new self-image is all about being wealthy, start acting wealthy. Don't worry, I'm not going to make you clear out your current bank balance on a designer handbag. No, that would be foolish, but you can wear your best clothes that make you feel wealthy, go to an expensive bar for *a* drink and savour the atmosphere, and then let your beautiful imagination run away with you.

I often walk to my office. Sometimes, if a bus is coming, I'll take it. As I say hello to the driver, I imagine he or she is my personal chauffeur, and off we go. It's fun; it amuses me, but as far as my subconscious is concerned, I'm loving the feeling of having my own personal driver.

If weight has been your challenge and your new self-image is a beautiful, constant size ten, say something positive to embed your new self-image every time you look in the mirror. Remember, you are reprograming her. Say things like, "Looking good, girl," or, "I can tell you've lost weight." No grimaces, sarcasm, or winces—just smiles and the belief everything is going in the right direction. You're feeling happy about the new you. Love the new you. If you are out with friends and they order cake and you would like a slice, have one. Recognise weight isn't a problem for you anymore. Enjoy the cake without guilt or remorse, just happiness. If you aren't happy eating cake, why would you eat it in the first place?

As mentioned before, download the free app Voice Loop, and record your new self-image. When you are recording, be positive, excited, and delighted to be this wonderful new woman. Listen to it daily when you are out and about. Enjoy hearing about you. This is a great way to reprogram your subconscious.

As you grow into this sparkling new woman, you will want to further enhance your self-image. Keep updating, re-writing, and re-recording. Feel it, believe it, behave it.

Enjoy the new you, the woman you were always meant to be. She is fabulous, and she is the best company you will ever have.

Chapter 8: Bringing the Fun Back

Well, hello! I am loving the new you. You look radiant. Isn't it so exciting to find *you* again and allowing her to shine?

How did it go defining your values?

What I found when I first did the values exercise was I had stopped living some of my values. I had somehow taken on the values of others that weren't really "me."

"Fun" was one such value. I had inadvertently dropped it from my life. How did that happen?

At the time, the company I was working for certainly didn't have "fun" as a corporate value. To top it off, my partner at the time didn't value fun. He thought it was rather frivolous and something I should have "grown out of by now."

I took drastic action. I left both my job and partner and travelled to Australia in search of fun and adventure. (It should be noted security and safety aren't my core values.)

I'm not saying everyone should take such drastic action, but given you have put such great effort into your new self-image and weaving in your values, ignore them at your own peril.

Create Your Life by Design, not by Default

Exercise:

Review your new self-image and see which aspects you are not yet fully living and which require more focus.

For example, even reviewing my self-image today, I am still looking for ways I can put more fun into my life or exhibit even more compassion. Here are a couple of simple goals I have set for myself around my declaration to behave according to my new self-image.

- Once a month, our family dinners will not be at home but out having fun. Each family member will take a turn choosing a fun thing to do, such as going "barefoot bowling" or out for a picnic.

- I will put loose coins in the front of my handbag to be easily accessible so I can donate to homeless people as I pass by. The money is really an ice-breaker to start a conversation, and that's where the real compassion begins.

By now, you will have begun listening closer to your intuition and not your self-talk—your Nasty Nan. The more you do so, the better. This is a daily practise, and each day will be different. Be aware, our self-talk is highly persistent and very, very, sneaky. Always be on guard for the rubbish she is ready to tell you at a moment's notice. If you have a bad day and your self-talk explodes, don't abandon your practise; instead, be kind to yourself.

With your new self-image in place, it is a perfect time to revisit your tasks both at work and home. What does the new you want to do? Can she carve out even more time by delegating, simplifying, and dumping? What are you going to do with that time?

One must is to bring more joy into your life, and that's not going to be by folding socks a certain way. No, there are better ways to bring yourself joy.

I am not going to be so glib as to say statements like, "Follow your passion, and the money will come." Firstly, there are way too many unemployed actors to prove this statement isn't necessarily true. Secondly, many of us just don't have a real passion. I mean, we like things, but wouldn't actually describe ourselves as being passionate about them.

Instead, think about what you love to do, both at work and play, and see how you can bring more of those elements into your life. If a new career or business evolves from that—wonderful! But for now, we are simply going to ensure you thrive by living by your values and doing more of what you love.

A girlfriend of mine in the UK, Clara, is experiencing a tsunami of stressors at the moment. Her mother has been diagnosed with early onset dementia, her husband is having scans for possible cancer, her teenage daughter has been dabbling with marijuana, and to top it off, it looks like her position in the company she works for is going to be removed with an impending restructure. Currently, wherever Clara turns, there's a challenge she can't fix, which is a nightmare. What is keeping her sane is her horse.

Clara started horse riding a couple of years ago. It was something she did as a child. She didn't start off passionate about it; it was just something to do to fill the void of not being needed as much as a hands-on mother. Three years later, riding has become an obsession; she's bought a horse and rides in local gymkhanas, even sleeping in the horse trailer despite her fear of spiders.

When she talks about horses, which is often, her face lights up, and her smile broadens. It brings her such joy, and I know it is this "fun stuff" helping her thrive at a time when life is proving so challenging.

We all need and deserve our own equivalent fun stuff— something that brings us joy, not only to keep us going in the tough times, but to simply bring more happiness into our lives (Melamed et al. 1995, 25-40).

So over to you. What do you love or enjoy doing?

Tricky, huh? Yes, after years of being busy with work, relationships, family, and putting everyone else first, it can be hard to come up with anything. Let me guide you.

Start writing your thoughts down to the following questions. As always, listen to your intuition, and keep Nasty Nan's annoying chatter at bay. Comments to look out for from your self-talk: "I'm too old to do that," "I can't afford it," or "People would think I'm crazy." Ignore her comments.

- What did you like to do as a child?
- If money was not an object, what would you do?
- What would your inner circle of friends and family say you enjoy?
- What are you good at? (We are often good at things we enjoy. Be mindful, though. We can also be good at things

we don't actually enjoy. Algebra would be one of mine; I just had a brilliant math teacher!)

- What do you never tire of reading about?
- What do you hate doing? (This can often trigger what we like doing.)
- What is something you have never tried that you have always dreamt of?
- If fear was removed, what would you do?

Review what you have written. Is there anything else to add? Compare with the activity list below. Is there anything on this list that sparks an interest?

Desire is the unexpressed possibility. If it's in you, it's possible.

Arts and Crafts Hobbies	Collecting	Profitable Hobbies
Baking	Figurines	Freelance writing/blogging
Journaling	Books	Crafting (to sell online or at fairs)
Digital art	Coins	Cake decorating
Cooking	Stamps	Garage sales and auctions (for resale)
Doll-making	Toys	Selling on eBay
Scrap-booking	Cars	Freelance photography
Knitting	Art	Carpentry
Crocheting	Tea spoons	Woodworking
Sewing	Autographs	Graphic design
Quilting	Antiques	Dressmaking
Book/movie club	Rocks and gems	Furniture restoration
Feng shui	Dolls	Interior design
Writing (short stories, poems, novels)	Snow globes	Couponing
Needlepoint		
Painting		
Drawing		
Indoor Hobbies	**Outdoor Hobbies**	**Hobbies to Sharpen the Mind**
Aquarium habitat building	Fishing	Jigsaw puzzles
	Biking	

Astronomy	Boating	Crossword puzzles
Astrology	Walking	Brain teasers
Pool	Hiking	Card games
Darts	Running	Chess
Ping-pong	Camping	Trivia contests
Yoga	Horse riding	Learn to draw, paint,
Pilates	Dancing	play an instrument or
	Swimming	speak a new language
	Gardening	
Team sports	**Adventure**	**My Ideas...**
Basketball	White water rafting	
Netball	RV-ing	
Soccer	Caving	
Football	Mountain climbing	
Tennis	Rock climbing	
Golf	Hot air balloon	
Baseball/softball	flying	
Volleyball	Gliding	
Coaching,	Parachuting	
officiating,	Surfing and	
reporting, and	windsurfing	
refereeing	Skiing/snowboarding	
Croquet	Scuba diving	
Bowling	Snorkelling	
Pickleball	Travel	

From your previous answers and this list, there should be some activities that sparked an interest. Don't overthink it. Just dive in. Remember, my girlfriend Clara didn't start out being passionate about horses; it was just something to do. My recommendation is:

- Try lots of activities.
- Experiment.
- Start small: hire or borrow equipment to see if you like it first.
- Follow your instincts and see where you go.
- Be brave and daring.

Spending more time doing things you enjoy will ensure you thrive. Create a plan of attack as to which ones you are going to start first.

As Nike says, "Just Do It."

We have nearly reached the end of the book, and there are just two final steps for you to take.

Now that you have connected with the new you, defined her in all her glory, what should she be doing in her next phase of life? Think bigger than the fun stuff; what do you want to do next?

Pause for a second and listen to your intuition. Your intuition knows the great potential you have and your heart's desires. What do you dream about? What have you always fancied doing? Don't worry about the "how" or listen to your self-talk. Instead, tap into your intuition and dream big!

Imagine you are sitting with me, and I have a magic wand. I can turn your dreams into reality. What would you do? Would you quit your job and sail around the world? Open up a café? Go back to university? Leave your partner? Find a new partner?

There are no limits. Dream away.

When a dream or fantasy comes to mind, I want you to capture your idea on paper.

Go bananas with this; throw caution to the wind and allow the sparkly new you to have a voice.

This dream or fantasy should be something you've never done before. It should excite you, make you a little nervous, and when we turn this dream of yours into a goal, you know it will make you grow.

If you are struggling to come up with your dream, flip to the index to visit my website and let me help you.

Let's explore how to turn this fantasy into a goal.

Write this fantasy as if it is a year from now and you have made everything in your dream come true. I want you to capture your new life in the present tense with as much detail as possible. Where are you writing this from? What is your new life like? How has the past year been? What have you achieved? What wonderful changes have you made? Who are you hanging around with? How are you spending your time? Start off your writing with the statement, "I am so happy and grateful I was brave, took control of my life, and made it my own. My life is so different now. I'm writing this from..."

Once you have created a vision of this exciting life goal, think of one action you could take today to move you closer to achieving it, even if it's a tiny step. Maybe do some research on the Internet or create a vision board. Every day, when you rewrite your goal, take another baby step towards it, then watch in awe over the coming weeks and months—suddenly, a plan is coming into place. This dream is turning into reality.

Each day, add more detail. Get more emotionally connected so you end up falling in love with your goal. Become delightfully obsessed with it.

Now that you have a delicious vision of your future, it is time to write a matching new "shopping list." This list captures all of the finer things in life you are worthy of receiving.

This is the grown-up version of writing a letter to Father Christmas, and I want you to approach this with the same optimism and joy a happy, healthy child would. This is to balance out our over-giving in life. It's time to think about what you would like and learn how to receive it.

You are going to write down all the things you would love in life from a loving partner, wonderful health, beautiful supportive family and friends, a successful business, lots of laughter, great travel experiences, a kitchen upgrade, Prada handbags, weekly massages, a weekly cleaner, regular haircuts, yoga retreat, time to simply *be*, flowers in the house, an Aston Martin DB11, fancy jewellery—it doesn't matter. This is a list of everything you can think of that would genuinely make you happy. Don't add things just for the sake of it; the list will lose its magic.

I want you to write as if *everything* is possible and you can have *anything* in life. Absolutely no self-talk allowed.

When you have written your wish list, I want you to look at the list and pick a couple of things you could allow yourself to receive right now. Go on; review your list. What stands out to you? Maybe the Aston Martin DB11 isn't quite in your price range yet, and that's okay, but what can you do for yourself right now? When I wrote my first "shopping list," it was for weekly massages and flowers. I realised I could make those happen now, and I do. Both are perfect reminders I'm worthy of whatever I desire. They make me feel special, and that is priceless.

Select your items and ***act on them now!***

Once you have your dream goal, and your best ever shopping list, it's time to accept these are now coming to you from the universe. You are worthy, you have put your order in, and more importantly, you are already taking daily action. Now, it's time to turn it over to the universe.

Have a ceremonial burning of both your dream life and wish list, sending them out into the universe with love and gratitude, and hold the belief that the universe will deliver to you.

I have loved having your company. I believe it is time for you to shine as the perfectly imperfect woman. Treasure this woman; she is priceless, and make sure you never lose sight of her again.

I want to leave you with this beautiful quote from the astrologer Rob Brezsny:

I am no longer looking for the perfect partner
to salve all my wounds
and fix all my mix-ups
and bridge all my chasms.
I am no longer looking for the perfect partner
because I am my own perfect partner.

Sending you love and happiness in being the exquisite woman you were always meant to be.

–Tracey

Index

"Two Roles" Vlog
https://traceyward.co/two-roles-2/

Book a free strategy call with Tracey or associate
https://calendly.com/tracey-ward/30min?month=2020-04

Helpline Table			
Australia	**UK**	**USA**	**Canada**
Lifeline 13 11 14 Lifeline has a national number to help put you in contact with a crisis service in your state. Anyone across Australia experiencing a personal crisis or thinking about suicide can call. www.lifeline. org.au	*Lifeline* 0808 808 8000 If you're at risk of self-harm or feeling anxious, telephone Lifeline. The helpline is confidential, free, and open 24/7. If you're concerned about a friend or family member, you can also contact Lifeline for advice. www.lifelinehel pline.info	*National Suicide Prevention Lifeline* 1-800-273-8255 Lifeline provides 24/7, free, and confidential support for prevention, crisis resources for you or your loved ones, and best practices for professionals and those in distress. www.suicidepr eventionlifelin e.org	*Canada Suicide Preventi on Service (CSPS)* Toll-free: 1-833-456-4566 Crisis Services Canada enables callers anywhere in Canada to access crisis support by phone in French or English. Available 24/7. www.crisisser vices.canada.c a
Beyond Blue 1300 224 636 Beyond Blue provides information and support to help everyone in Australia achieve their	*Samaritans* 116 123 (free 24-hr helpline) Confidential support for people experiencing feelings of distress or	*The Samaritans* (877) 870-4673 (HOPE) If you are feeling uncertain about anything in your life, you will get help	*Crisis Support Services* 1800 273 8255 Contact for free, confidential support at any time, 365 days a year.

best possible mental health, whatever their age and wherever they live. www.Beyond blue.org.au	despair. www.samaritan s.org.uk	from a trained volunteer offering non-judgmental support no matter the reason. https://samarita nshope.org/our -services/247-crisis-services/	They're always available. https://cssnv.o rg/
1800 Respect 1800 737 732 1800RESPE CT are open 24 hours to support people impacted by sexual assault, domestic or family violence and abuse. www.1800re spect.org.au	*SupportLine* 01708 765200 SupportLine offers confidential emotional support particularly aimed at those who are isolated, at risk, vulnerable, and victims of any form of abuse www.supportlin e.org.uk	*National Domestic Violence Hotline* 1800 799 7233 For anyone affected by abuse and needing support. www.thehotlin e.org	*Assaulted Women's Helpline* 1866 863 0511 A free, anonymous and confidential 24-hour telephone and TTY crisis telephone line to all women who have experienced any form of abuse. http://www.a whl.org/

Acknowledgements

Where do I start?

This book originally was an online program. Adam, my business partner, helped me be brave in putting that together, Chris helped me find my writing voice, Janet tidied up my initial writing, Lisa and Linda came up with great phrases like "oxygen suckers" and "muzzle your inner bitch," Kellie chivied me along with encouragement, and Penny and Anna were super patient and went through lots of iterations and ideas often over several glasses of wine.

To all the beautiful women who ploughed through the online course and gave me their honest feedback, thank you; hence it's a book now and not a program. They say feedback is a gift, and they're right.

Erica and Chrissy and the team at Write my Wrongs—the editing transformation was magical. I always knew what I wanted to say, but putting pen to paper is much more difficult.

Thank you to Vicky for helping me find the title.

And finally, thanks to my beautiful mother, who was the inspiration for the book. Wherever you are in the spiritual world, Mum, I hope this book makes you proud. Thanks to my two beautiful children who hate reading and are unlikely to ever read this book but provide great inspiration and joy for me on a daily basis nevertheless.

About Tracey Ward

Growing up as the only child of a single working mother in the '60s and '70s, Tracey was well aware of the pressure on her mother to keep them afloat. She watched her mother sacrifice her own well-being daily as she looked after elderly parents, a lively daughter, and an unruly dog, while working full-time to pay all the bills and run a home.

Tracey learnt two important lessons: women can do just about anything, and women can easily lose themselves between work, home, and the fifth load of laundry.

Tracey's purpose with this book is to help beautiful women like her mother who give so much to everyone else but not to themselves. *Being Perfectly Imperfect* is designed to help women discover—or even rediscover—their true selves by learning to value who they are on the inside and surround themselves with good people, while still making time for fun in their busy lives.

A coach for over twenty-five years, Tracey has a unique mix of frankness, care, humour, and honesty that inspires women of all ages to go for the things they really want in life, to reach their full potential, and live their dreams—or simply get to watch the Netflix show they really want to see! Small wins are really important in life.

Tracey has a Graduate Diploma in Psychology and an Honours Degree in Civil Engineering. But, if you ask what her greatest achievements are in life, she would say: raising two children who are still lovely and inspiring in their late teens and managing an amicable divorce after twenty years. It truly is an achievement list that makes Tracey Ward one unique woman.

***

This is what other women have to say about Tracey Ward:

"Tracey is the best kept secret I have ever invested in. Professional development training for one's self is often put to the bottom of the priority list as it can be quite confronting—until you meet Tracey Ward. Working with Tracey this year has been pivotal in my career as a female CEO in the IT industry, frequently needing to engage in 'real' conversations. Tracey's smart yet practical techniques and superior insight into how we interact with each other in the changing workforce has been invaluable in driving my successful outcomes. Her intelligent, humorous, and insightful coaching style left me feeling each session ended too quickly and it was time to bring out the coffee and biscuits and solve all the world's problems!"
Nicki Page CEO, NED, Digital Transformation, Technology Innovation, Storyteller, Thought Leader & Industry Advocate

"Tracey is a highly skilled executive coach and an excellent communicator. I recently sought her expertise to improve my ability to deal with difficult professional and personal

conversations. I have benefited greatly from Tracey's professional, empathetic, and very practical input. Tracey shared with me several communication strategies that have tangibly improved the quality of my interactions with others. In particular, through using Tracey's strategies, I have noticed my communication style has become less 'reactive' and more 'proactive.' I highly recommend Tracey's professional coaching and communication expertise and experience."
Karen Watts, PhD

"I was stuck; I knew I wanted to return to work after some years off raising my children. I had a good idea of what I did not want to do (return to the law or investment banking) but was unclear about what I did want to do. Tracey led me through a powerful self-exploration process that literally 'unstuck' me. I am now enjoying my new work on a board, have another board appointment, and I am clear and happy about the direction I am heading in. I am immensely grateful to Tracey."
Andrea Gardiner, Jelix Ventures, founder and board director

"Tracey delighted us with her keynote on presentation skills to an audience of eighty people, most of whom thought they knew everything there was to know about presentation skills. She practised what she preached, she engaged and inspired us to change, it was educational and very entertaining, and I would highly recommend her to speak at any event. She will help make that event really successful."
Kimberley Daley, Head of Forensic Advisory Services (Australia) Sedgwick

"Tracey is a superb facilitator. She is professional, knows her stuff, and connects with participants to provide a rich learning environment. She combines real life stories and experience with theory as well as personality and humour. I can highly recommend Tracey as a quality facilitator."
Marisa Dantanarayana, Director, Footprint Coaching and Consulting

"We recently worked with Tracey to help our Women in Engineering group build confidence and capability in their communication styles. Tracey did a fantastic job of outlining what to be aware of when communicating with the opposite gender, and more importantly, provided some really simple solutions and alternatives to use to drive better outcomes. In a short span of time, with high energy and a lot of laughs, Tracey was able to provide our group with some practical tools to take action and bring about positive change in their interactions. Great feedback from the participants as well."
Melinda Small, Organisational Development Manager, Qantas

"Tracey is a coach who gives you great value the moment you engage her. Her friendly style means you warm to her instantly, your barriers are down, and issues are overcome and resolved. Tie that with her no-nonsense approach means Tracey gets you into action, quickly helping you achieve goals often higher than you thought possible."
Kellie King, Head of Lean Transformation, Bupa

"Having just been offered the daunting task to MC for the first time at a large industry conference, I knew I needed help in preparing for the event. Tracey led me on a wonderful journey of self-awareness around my existing presentation, delivery, and communication style which, much to my dislike at first, involved being recorded. This technique paid off tenfold as I was able to see first-hand how I came across to an audience and the areas I needed to work on. Tracey taught me the differences between being a presenter and an MC along with so many techniques and strategies to use in my delivery. Together, we worked on everything from stage positioning and material to delivery and even what to wear for the event. Tracey set me up for success and was there to support me even through the rehearsals for the event. I recently performed my MC duties. Not only am I grateful I stepped out of my comfort zone but also that I was introduced to Tracey as my coach. I have incorporated so many of these new techniques into the way I go about presenting and communicating and feel much more confident in my ability when in these situations. Tracey is the ultimate professional. She is talented,

honest, engaging, and so much fun to work with."
Christine Bell, QBE Regional Manager

Bibliography

Brown, Lydia, Christina Bryant, Valerie Brown, Bei Bei, and
    Fiona Judd. "Investigating How Menopausal Factors and
    Self-Compassion Shape Well-Being: An Exploratory Path
    Analysis." *Maturitas* 81, no. 2 (June 2015): 293–99.
    https://doi.org/10.1016/j.maturitas.2015.03.001.

Chapman, Gary. *The 5 Love Languages: The Secret to Love that
    Lasts.* Chicago, IL: Northfield Publishing, 2015.

Goleman, Daniel. "The Experience of Touch: Research Points to a
    Critical Role." *The New York Times*, February 2, 1988.
    *https://www.nytimes.com/1988/02/02/science/the-
    experience-of-touch-research-points-to-a-critical-role.html.*

Jacobson, Sheri, ed. "Generous Person, or Over-Giver? (And At
    What Cost If So?)." *Harley Therapy Counselling Blog.*
    Harley Therapy, March 20, 2018.
    *https://www.harleytherapy.co.uk/counselling/generous-
    person-or-over-giver.htm.*

Jeffery, Scott. "Core Values List: Over 200 Personal Values to
    Live By Today." CEOsage, February 18, 2020.
    https://scottjeffrey.com/core-values-list/.

Lieberman, Daniel E. "Is Exercise Really Medicine? An
    Evolutionary Perspective." *Current Sports Medicine
    Reports* 14, no. 4 (2015): 313–19.
    https://doi.org/10.1249/jsr.0000000000000168.

Light, Kathleen C., Karen M. Grewen, and Janet A. Amico. "More
    Frequent Partner Hugs and Higher Oxytocin Levels Are
    Linked to Lower Blood Pressure and Heart Rate in
    Premenopausal Women." *Biological Psychology* 69, no. 1
    (April 2005): 5–21.
    https://doi.org/10.1016/j.biopsycho.2004.11.002.

Maltz, Maxwell. *Psycho-Cybernetics*. Waco, TX: Success Motivation Institute, 1960.

Mcbeath, V. L. "Women's Rights: Not Up for Discussion." VL McBeath. Accessed April 20, 2020. *https://valmcbeath.com/victorian-era-womens-rights/#.XpkVINMzbBJ.*

Melamed, Samuel, Elchanan I. Meir, and Amit Samson. "The Benefits of Personality-Leisure Congruence: Evidence and Implications." *Journal of Leisure Research* 27, no. 1 (January 1, 1995): 25–40. *https://doi.org/10.1080/00222216.1995.11969975.*

Neff, Kristin D., Kristin L. Kirkpatrick, and Stephanie S. Rude. "Self-Compassion and Adaptive Psychological Functioning." *Journal of Research in Personality* 41, no. 1 (February 2007): 139–54. *https://doi.org/10.1016/j.jrp.2006.03.004.*

Puchalsky, Andrea. "Holiday Tip: Most Americans Say Social Conversations About Money Are Taboo, According to Ally Bank's Money Talks Study." Ally, November 24, 2015. *https://media.ally.com/2015-11-24-Holiday-Tip-Most-Americans-Say-Social-Conversations-About-Money-are-Taboo-According-to-Ally-Banks-Money-Talks-Study.*

Quinn, Elizabeth. "Why Athletes Need Rest and Recovery After Exercise." Verywell Fit. Verywell Fit, January 6, 2020. *https://www.verywellfit.com/the-benefits-of-rest-and-recovery-after-exercise-3120575.*

Schroeder-Gardner, Michelle. "Why Do People Hate Talking About Money?" Making Sense Of Cents, November 26, 2018. *https://www.makingsenseofcents.com/2017/06/talking-about-money.html.*

"What Is Financial Abuse?" White Ribbon Australia. White
Ribbon Australia. Accessed 2020.
https://www.whiteribbon.org.au/understand-domestic-
violence/types-of-abuse/financial-abuse/.

2015 Couples Retirement Study Fact Sheet. Fidelity Investments,
2015. *https://www.fidelity.com/bin-
public/060_www_fidelity_com/documents/couples-
retirement-fact-sheet.pdf.*

www.ingramcontent.com/pod-product-compliance
Lightning Source LLC
Chambersburg PA
CBHW060042030426
42334CB00019B/2452

9 7 8 0 6 4 8 8 2 5 5 0 0